EMILY POST'S
THE GUIDE TO GOOD MANNERS FOR KIDS

Emily Post's

THE GUIDE TO

GOOD
MANNERS
for Kids

BY PEGGY POST
&
CINDY POST SENNING, ED.D.

HarperCollins*Publishers*

We dedicate this book to all kids everywhere!

We acknowledge with deep appreciation the following people for their support and contributions to this book:

Our junior advisory board who spent time with us reviewing the table of contents, reading chapters, and offering suggestions from their point of view: Laura Bataille, fourth grade, Thatcher Brook Primary School, Waterbury, Vermont; Analina Aitken, sixth grade, Crossett Brook Middle School, Duxbury, Vermont; Gabriela Meade, sixth grade, Crossett Brook Middle School, Duxbury, Vermont; Samantha Pheffer, sixth grade, Crossett Brook Middle School, Duxbury, Vermont; Alex Houston, fifth and sixth grade teacher at Crossett Brook Middle School, for her time and guidance to the junior advisory group.

Mark McVeigh and Meghan Dietsche of HarperCollins Children's Books for their creativity, help, and attention to detail throughout the writing and production of the book.

Katherine Cowles, Elizabeth Howell, and Peter Post for their many suggestions, creative advice, and invaluable assistance. We couldn't have done it without them!

And, as always, the legacy of Emily Post, whose generosity of spirit and timeless wisdom serves as a foundation for this and every book written in her name.

Emily Post's The Guide to Good Manners for Kids
Text copyright © 2004 by Peggy Post and Cindy Post Senning
Illustrations copyright © 2004 by Steve Björkman

For information address HarperCollins Children's Books,
a division of HarperCollins Publishers, 1350 Avenue of the Americas, New York, NY 10019.
www.harperchildrens.com

Library of Congress Cataloging-in-Publication Data
Post, Peggy.
    Emily Post's the guide to good manners for kids / by Peggy Post and Cindy Post
Senning, Ed.D.— 1st ed.
        p.   cm.
    ISBN 0-06-057196-9 — ISBN 0-06-057197-7 (lib. bdg.)
    1. Etiquette for children and teenagers [1. Etiquette. 2. Behavior.] I. Title: Guide to good
manners for kids. II. Senning, Cindy Post. III. Björkman, Steve. IV. Title.
BJ1857.C5P66 2004   2003026426
395.1'22—dc22

Typography by Jeanne L. Hogle
7   8   9   10
❖
First Edition

CONTENTS

INTRODUCTION

WHY MANNERS?

Back in eighteenth-century France, King Louis XIV used to invite people to his palace for parties and festivals. However, he became really upset when people walked all over the lawns and gardens, squishing the grass and stomping on flowers. So before the next party, he called in his gardener to talk about this problem. They decided to put up little signs everywhere saying: Please don't walk on the flowers! Stay on the path. Be careful of the roses. The signs guided the guests so they would know where it was okay to walk and where it wasn't. The word in French for the little signs was "etiquette." Over time the word *etiquette* came to mean all the little signs that help us know what to do in new and different situations. And, in even more time, etiquette came to mean all the things we do to help us get along better with those we meet in our daily lives.

Today the little signs make up the set of manners we think of as etiquette. They say things such as, "Say please and thank you." "Take off your hat when you come to the table, please." "Don't read your sister's mail." "Please help clear the table." "When your friends come over, remember to introduce them to your parents." Etiquette, or manners, guide you through all of your activities. Each little sign is like a tool to help you get along. And just as with all tools, you need to learn how to use them. It takes practice, practice, practice. . . .

This book is for you. It will tell you the manners you need to know and how to use them. It will tell you about manners for

+ **Getting along with others.** Manners are an essential ingredient in the glue that holds families together. You'll discover manners that will strengthen your relationships not only with your family but also with friends, teachers, and the other people you meet every day.

+ **Helping you get through the day more easily**—wherever you are. You'll learn about manners that will guide you through the mall and your school, on planes or trains, at parties, in a taxi, during a hospital visit, or at a service in a church or synagogue.

+ **Knowing what to expect in new and different situations.** If you're invited to be in a wedding or to go to a bar mitzvah, you'll find the manners that will help you know how to act and what to expect.

What happens when it seems the manners you know don't fit a specific situation? Or maybe it's impossible to learn all the manners necessary and you're in a situation where you don't know what to do. All you need to do is apply some basic ideas. Ask yourself how you can be *respectful, considerate,* and *honest.* In most situations, just think about how you would like to be treated, and you'll have the answer you need! Or, maybe, you can find the answer by asking someone else.

Three principles are the basis of all the manners in this book:

✦ **Respect means caring for and understanding others** just as they are—their culture, their habits, and their strengths and weaknesses. Showing respect means acting toward people with care and understanding for them.

✦ **Consideration just means thinking about other people.** It's thinking about how what you are doing will affect them.

✦ **Honesty is more than just not telling lies.** It is finding the truth and then telling it. And if the truth might be hurtful, it's finding a way to put the truth in a positive light. When your mother asks, "Don't you like the carrots?" instead of saying, "They are yucky!" which might be the truth, you could say, "Carrots aren't my favorite vegetable, but the chicken was great!"—also the truth.

No matter what the situation is or where you find yourself, if you choose to act with respect, consideration, and honesty you will do well. Your relationships with your family and friends will be better. And while sometimes being considerate, respectful, or honest seems as if it just benefits the other person, it will benefit you, too. You will feel better about yourself just for helping someone else have a better day or treating them the way you would want to be treated.

Learn to use the manners in this book and you will have the tools you need to get through difficult situations more easily. You'll know what to expect in so many more situations, and you'll have more confidence for facing new ones. Take advantage of this gift of good manners and you will develop a sense of self-respect and self-confidence that will make your day and the day of everyone around you just a little bit better.

CHAPTER ONE

EVERYDAY LIFE
WINNING WITH WORDS

" The way you use words has an effect on every relationship you have. "

Perhaps you are the quiet type. Or maybe you like to talk a lot. In either case, the way you use words will affect how well you get along with your friends and family. You don't have to be great at talking with people, but you do have to choose your words carefully to smooth your way. Whether you're talking to your grandparents or your best friend—whether it is one word or hours of conversation—your choice of words, your ability to string them together effectively, and your use of your vocabulary will make all the difference in your relationships.

Great conversations require more than choosing the right words. Your facial expressions and body language play a big part, too. If you are feeling good about what you are saying, make sure you have a smile on your face. If you are serious about the conversation, don't shrug or appear bored. If the topic is a sad one, don't pepper your conversation with giggles. A carefully timed "eye roll" or a drawn out "Excuuuse me" can change the whole meaning of a conversation—and not always for the better.

BASIC MANNERS

Beyond the "Magic Words"

CONSIDER THIS: You're walking down a crowded hallway in school and someone crashes into you. He or she may grunt and move on or may say, "Excuse me—are you okay?" Wouldn't "excuse me" make you feel better? If you already have "please" and "thank you" down pat, it's time to add several new "magic words" to your manners vocabulary:

✦ **"You're welcome"** is the third in the trio of classic magic words.

✦ **"Excuse me"** can be used in many situations, including bumping into someone or interrupting. It shows consideration, no matter what the situation.

✦ **"No, thank you"** is a great improvement over a solitary "No" or "Eew, I don't like that stuff!"

✦ **"Hi, how are you?"** is a friendly greeting that will start things off on the right foot. (And a quick reply of "Fine, thanks. How are you?" will keep the conversation going.)

✦ **"Can I . . . ?"** It's always nicer to ask than to demand. (Just be prepared for the correction, "Do you mean, 'May I . . . ?'")

The Art of Conversation

CONSIDER THIS: There's a new kid in your class you really want to meet. You're the last one to get on the bus and the only seat is next to this kid. You sit down. Now what? Just start—"Hi, my name is Sam. You're Billy, aren't you? How are things going for you at school so far?" You can ask questions to help you get acquainted with each other. Or, you can move on to what are called safe topics: the weather, sports, the latest great song by a popular music group, the recent play at the school—and you're off. The important things to remember are

  ✦ **Show interest**—ask questions, make comments, listen carefully.

  ✦ **Look at the person** who's speaking.

  ✦ **Pay attention** to what he says—don't spend your time thinking about what you'll say next or you won't hear what he says first.

  ✦ **Don't interrupt.**

  ✦ **Speak clearly** with a lively tone of voice when it's your turn.

  ✦ **End the conversation pleasantly** when the bus reaches your stop.

This will happen before you know it if you are enjoying the conversation.

Whether it's talking to the kid on the bus, speaking to your grandmother on the phone, or just chatting with your mom or best friend, the same principles apply. If you practice them in conversations with people you know well, you'll be a natural in any setting. You'll also have some great dinner table conversations with your family or at your friend's house and will be more comfortable in discussion groups in class.

If you are feeling good about what you are saying, make sure you have a smile on your face.

WHAT IF?
MULTIPLE CHOICE

WHAT IF . . . *You're with a bunch of kids. They start saying mean things about a classmate. What should you do?*

WOULD YOU . . .

1. Join in and say a few mean things yourself?

2. Excuse yourself from the conversation? "Sorry, gotta go to dinner. See you later."

3. Put in some good words about the classmate and change the whole conversation? "Yeah, but did you know that Ellie actually goes rock climbing on weekends with her dad? She has some amazing stories about climbing."

CORRECT ANSWER: *3. The way you steer the conversation will set the mood for the rest of the time you and your friends are together. Moving the talk to a more positive level requires a little thought, practice, and some guts. But you can take control. You can set the tone. And all you have to do is pay attention to your choice of words.*

ALWAYS:

✦ Use those magic words.

✦ Listen "actively" (pay attention, look at the person).

✦ Choose and use the words that say what you mean.

✦ Be a part of the conversation.

✦ Include everyone in the group.

✦ End conversations nicely ("Sorry, I gotta go now—dinnertime!").

✦ Avoid phrases that just fill empty space; for example, "Like, you know what I mean?" or "Uhhh" or "Ya know?"

NEVER:

✦ Skip "please" and "thank you" because it seems cool—it isn't.

✦ Talk just to hear yourself talk.

✦ Use slang that's okay with your friends with your grandmother (while some slang is okay, be careful where you use it).

✦ Use foul language with anybody—even your friends. It reflects badly on you and can be a hard habit to break.

RESPECTFUL WORDS FOR FAMILY AND FRIENDS

The way you use words has an effect on every relationship you have. Your friends want to be treated with respect. If you ask rather than demand, they will be glad to give you a hand. Your family wants to be treated with respect, too. If you show interest in what's important to them, they'll return that interest. The use of appropriate language shows respect, and respect is the foundation of good relationships. Use your words well.

THE WRITTEN WORD

A handwritten note has its own special magic. Have you ever held a letter or card in your hands, reading and rereading the words? Did you appreciate the care, time, and effort that went into writing and mailing the letter? Letters can help you connect with people in a way that you don't with e-mail and phone conversations.

Because it takes time, thought, and special materials to write a letter, we often take the

WE GET LETTERS . . . OR DO WE?

PICTURE THIS: *You are at camp. Mail call! The counselor passes out the mail. Either you will be psyched to get a letter from your best friend or you will feel let down when there is no mail for you. If you didn't get a letter, is there anything you can do about it? Yes. If you want to get letters, you've got to write letters. Everyone loves getting mail, and most people like responding to a friendly, well-written letter.*

easy way out. A quick phone call to a friend who has moved away can substitute for a letter. An e-mail to your aunt who sent a birthday gift meets the obligation of thanking her. But a call or an e-mail does not show the care and affection that a written note does.

Use Your Imagination

It's not easy to write a letter. One way to figure out what to say in a letter is to imagine you're in a conversation with the person you are writing to. Simply write down what you would say if the person were sitting in the room with you. Imagine what might be of special interest to her. For example, if you're writing to your good friend who moved away and shopping was something you loved to do together, tell her about the new store that just opened at your favorite mall.

Write a Letter

How do you become a good letter writer? Practice! The more you write, the better your letters will be. The first one is always the hardest. Think of someone special and write a letter using the following guidelines:

✦ **Start with the date.**

✦ **Next comes a greeting**—the most common one is "Dear . . ."

✦ Make sure you **spell the name of the person correctly.** Using the correct spelling shows respect for the person you are writing.

✦ Make sure you **have the correct address** and be sure to include your return address. It would be a shame to take the time to write the letter and then have it sit in the dead-letter file at the post office.

✦ **Write neatly!** The person you are writing to will want to be able to read it.

✦ Before you begin writing, **think about what you have to say** and what the person you are writing to would be interested in. Always include two or three things the person would care about. Ask questions that show your interest in him or her. Let the person know you are looking forward to seeing him or her again.

✦ **Sign it.** Use a closing that fits your relationship. "Love" is for family and close friends. "Yours truly" works for just about everybody. Maybe you would feel more comfortable with "Your friend."

✦ **Send it.** Keep a few stamps with your writing supplies so you can just drop the letter in a mailbox. The post office has a great variety of stamps available. Stop by and select some you especially like.

> ## THREE TIPS TO HELP MAKE LETTER WRITING EASY
>
> 1. *Keep a dictionary handy* so you can easily check the spelling for any word you're not sure of.
> 2. *Read what you have written* out loud. If it's easy to read and you don't stumble, it's ready to go.
> 3. *Address it,* stamp it, and put it in the mailbox right away!

RESPECTING PRIVACY

Letters are private! A sealed letter is confidential and should be read only by the person it is mailed to. In days of old, people even sealed their letters with a personal mark set in colored wax to ensure that it hadn't been opened while it was en route.

Three Important Nevers

- ✦ Never open mail addressed to someone else.
- ✦ Never read someone else's mail without the person's permission.
- ✦ Never share a letter with others if someone has written something to you in confidence.

BEYOND THE LETTER

The Postcard

Tokyo, Paris, the Caribbean, San Francisco, Mexico, Ireland, fall foliage in Vermont, skiing in Colorado, art museums in Chicago . . . You can't bring all your friends and family with you, but you can share your trip with them. Send a postcard, share your adventures. Remember, though—a postcard is not the place for private messages. Everyone can read it.

The Greeting Card

Birthday cards, get-well cards, congratulations, good luck, bon voyage . . . You name it, there is a greeting card for any occasion. Greeting cards can be funny, pretty, sentimental, a little rude, and more. Choose your card wisely. Read it from the point of view of the person you will send it to (the card is for the person, not you), and add a note to make it special.

FAMILY AND FRIENDS

In this age of electronic communications, letters stand out. They will make your relationships just a little more special. Think about how much you enjoy getting something in the mail. Maybe your brother has gone off to college, your sister has joined the service, your grandmother has moved into a nursing home, your best friend moved to another state, a favorite teacher is now teaching in a different school. All of these people would love to hear from you. They want to know what you are doing. They will read and reread your letter. Maybe a phone call is easier, but a letter creates a bond between you and the recipient that will last as long as the letter does.

THANK YOU

Thanking people is our way of respecting them by showing appreciation. A thoughtful thank-you makes us appear considerate and appreciative. On the other hand, not thanking a person makes us appear inconsiderate and unappreciative. Consider this: If you think someone is inconsiderate or unappreciative, are you likely to want him or her as a friend? Because thank-yous are SO important there are actually rules to help you know when to write thank-you notes.

JOURNALS HELP TO BUILD THE WRITING HABIT

PICTURE THIS: *You spend three weeks visiting the national parks in Utah, Wyoming, and Arizona. Each night you write down in a journal the sights you saw, the foods you ate, any special activities you did. In September when you need to write a report about your summer, you will have all the information in one place.*

Journals can be used to record your thoughts, activities, special events, ideas, and emotions. You can keep one every day for a year or just for special times—like trips or a two-week session at camp. They can be private or can be shared with others. Journals give you practice in writing and help you build all the habits that make good writers.

ALWAYS:

✦ Write a thank-you note when you receive a gift and the giver is not there to receive your thanks in person (such as when someone sends you a gift in the mail or asks someone else to bring a gift to your party when he or she can't come). Your thank-you note not only tells the person how much you appreciate the gift, it lets him or her know it arrived.

✦ Write a thank-you note when you have been a houseguest at someone's home. (Exception: Sometimes you just go for an overnight to your best friend's house. You don't need to write a thank-you for that, but if you stay more than one night or you travel to a friend's house out of town for a special event, you should write a thank-you note.)

✦ Write and send a thank-you as quickly as possible—within a day or two of receiving the gift or returning home from the visit.

NOT REQUIRED BUT NICE:

✦ Write a thank-you note even if you've thanked the giver in person— especially if it was given at a big party and your personal thanks might have been lost in the excitement.

✦ Write a thank-you note when someone has done something special for you—such as when your uncle made a big effort to get to your championship game and cheered you on like crazy.

NEVER:

✦ Skip writing a thank-you note just because you're embarrassed that it's been a week and the note might be late.

✦ Use preprinted thank-you notes where you just have to fill in the blanks. The impersonal look of those cards takes away from the thought you might have put into the thank-you.

ON THE JOB

Just because you don't get a paycheck doesn't mean you don't have a job. The chores you do to help keep the household running smoothly are a job. Every day that you go to school, you are on the job—the job of learning. You may shovel snow, rake lawns, do errands for an elderly neighbor, baby-sit, deliver newspapers, or walk some dogs. All these jobs have three things in common:

- ✦ They involve **working with others**.
- ✦ They involve the **acceptance of some responsibility** on your part.
- ✦ There are **manners that guide our behavior** while doing them.

Let's consider a few!

Baby-sitting: As the baby-sitter, you have a responsibility to both the child and the parents. You are taking on the responsibility of care for that child during the parents' absence. The parents make plans based on what you've agreed to do—such as showing up at four o'clock, feeding the baby, or making sure the kids take a bath and go to bed on time. Using good manners in this situation requires being on time, treating the children with respect, doing the things you've agreed to, talking to the parents courteously, focusing on the job at hand (not talking to your friends on the phone), and treating the home you are in with respect. Do these things well and both the kids and the parents will want you to baby-sit again.

Shoveling a walk: It is your responsibility to be sure the walkway is clear and safe. The basic manners include finishing the job by the agreed-upon time, doing a good job of it, focusing on the job (not bringing three of your friends and having a snowball fight while you're working), and talking to the walkway's owner in a respectful tone. Do it well and you will have a job for the winter and an employer who will recommend you to other people.

Chores at home: Timeliness, focus, and maintaining a respectful tone are just as important when doing a job at home as they are when doing a paying job in the neighborhood. Do your chores well and you will discover parents and brothers and sisters who appreciate you and who may be more likely to go out of their way to help you.

ALWAYS:

◆ Be on time for your job and do your work in a timely fashion.

◆ Talk respectfully to your employer and to anyone associated with your work.

◆ Focus on the job at hand.

◆ Dress appropriately.

◆ Do the job exactly as you agreed to.

NEVER:

◆ Cancel a job just because something comes up that would be more fun.

◆ Bring along your friends because sometimes the job can be boring.

◆ Use bad language.

◆ Do the job halfway—your work reflects on you and will determine how people think of you in the future.

A QUESTION *for* PEGGY & CINDY

QUESTION: *I baby-sit regularly for a family who always leaves a big mess for me to clean up. I am there to watch the kids, not to do housework. What can I say?*

ANSWER: *The next time this family asks you to baby-sit, tell them you would like to but you have something you want to talk about. Then explain that having to do the housework distracts you from the important part of the job—watching* *the kids. Tell them that it is important for you to do the best job you can making sure their kids have a safe, enjoyable evening, but that housework keeps you from it. You might offer to do the dishes you use while you are there, but you are not on board to clean house; you are there to watch the kids!*

THE CHOICE IS YOURS . . .

Sometimes work is boring. There is nothing exciting about washing that one hundredth dish.

Sometimes work is gross. Does anyone really like changing a diaper, cleaning up puppy poop, or taking out the garbage?

Sometimes work is not what you want to be doing. You would much rather go to the beach with your friends than work in the yard with your family.

It has been said that if work was always enjoyable, they wouldn't have to pay people to do it. Sometimes when we've committed to doing something, it's not exactly what we would like to do. This is where responsibility comes into play. When you agree to do a job, someone—family, friend, or neighbor—is counting on you. How you tackle the job will affect that person's opinion of you. You will develop a reputation as either responsible or irresponsible. That reputation will follow you for a long time. The choice is yours . . . both the choice about what to do and the choice about what your reputation will be.

You decide what attitude you bring to the job. The expression on your face, the tone of your voice, the pace of your work will affect everyone's day. How you act on the job will determine whether or not you get the job the next time. Your relationships on the job are every bit as important as your social relationships. As you do the chores and jobs you get as a kid, you will develop work habits that will serve you either ill or well throughout your life. The choice is yours. What will it be?

HI! HOW ARE YOU?

You get only one chance to make a first impression! Greeting others, making introductions, and introducing yourself can be awkward, and especially if you are shy, somewhat embarrassing. Here is where etiquette comes to your rescue. Half the battle is knowing *how* to introduce someone; the other half is being familiar with some greetings that you're comfortable using. It's always easier when you know what the other person is going to do and what is expected of you.

GREETINGS

Greetings can be as simple as a quick "Good morning" to the bus driver or as complicated as trying to remember the names of everybody in a group of people you've only just met. Here are some basics that apply to greetings:

+ **Stand up**—if you are seated.
+ **Smile!**
+ **Look the person** you're greeting in the eye.
+ **Move toward him or her** and offer a handshake if it's someone you're meeting for the first time.
+ **If you're greeting an adult you know** but don't see often, you have some choices: you would either shake her hand and do nothing more, or give a hug (if it's your grandmother, aunt, or someone else you're close to).
+ **Say the person's name** as part of the greeting. "Hello, Mr. Driver" or "Hi, Tom."

◆ **When you greet your friends** or someone you see on a daily basis (your teacher, for instance), you do not need to stand or shake hands. But do come up with some friendly greeting, even if it's just a "Hi!"

◆ Unless it really is just a quick "Hello," **be ready with a follow-up** such as "How are you?" or "Great day, isn't it?"

◆ When the other person says "Hi" to you, **respond with your own "Hi"** and maybe a brief comment like "How are you?"

> # THE BASICS—
> # A HANDSHAKE
>
> 1. *Extend* your right hand—thumb up, palm flat.
> 2. *Grasp* the hand firmly palm to palm (avoid the bone crunch or the limp rag).
> 3. *Pump* your hand two or three times.
> 4. *Release.*

The idea is to make the other people feel welcome and to give the impression that you are glad to see them. You don't need to repeat all these steps every time you see someone or a visitor to your home walks into the room.

In the case of adult visitors to your home . . . if they have left for a while and then returned, your greeting can be briefer and more informal. Even though you do not need to stand or shake hands every time they return to the house, it is respectful to stop what you are doing, greet them on their return, and show some interest. "Hi, Dad and Mr. Donelli. How was your golf game?" Then return to what you were doing.

Mr., Mrs., Ms, Dr., or First Names

Depending on how well you know the adult, how old you are, and what they prefer, you may call adults by their proper title (and last name) or their first name. How do you know? The guideline here is really very simple. *You address adults by their title and last name—unless they specifically ask you to use their first name or something else.* If you are introducing someone your age to an adult, you use the adult's title and last name. You then let the adult make the choice whether or not to request something different. "Aunt Molly, this is my friend Samantha. Sam, this is my aunt Molly, Mrs. Richards." Your aunt may then choose to say, "Hi, Sam, please feel free to call me Molly. All the kids do." Or, she might simply say hello to Sam and not comment on her name, meaning that she wants Sam to call her Mrs. Richards.

INTRODUCTIONS (OR TRADING NAMES)

Introducing people is one of the most important etiquette skills you will learn. Many people think it is complicated and confusing so they don't do it. Then people are left in that awkward position of not knowing whom they are talking to. Really, introductions are not that difficult. At the most basic level, making an introduction is just trading names. Whether you are introducing yourself or introducing two people you know who have never met each other, or you are being introduced to someone, the goal of the introduction is for all involved to know who is who.

"Uncle Bob, this is my friend Joe. We're in the school play together. Joe, this is my uncle Bob, Mr. Heath."

There is a basic form to introductions no matter what the situation.

ALWAYS:

✦ Stand, smile, and shake hands (just as in a greeting).

✦ Look the person in the eye.

✦ Introduce the younger person to the older person first. The trick here is to say the older person's name first. "Mrs. Smith, this is my friend Mary." "Grandmother, I want you to meet my teacher, Mrs. English." If it is not clear who is older, then it doesn't make much difference as long as you trade names.

✦ Pronounce names clearly.

✦ Use an adult's title and last name. "Mom, this is my coach, Miss Whales." (If the adult prefers to be called by her first name, she can say so.)

✦ When you know it, include a little description that helps people understand the connections. "Jackie, this is my coach, Miss Whales. She's the one I told you about who has a great trick for making foul shots."

✦ Make the introduction even if you've forgotten the person's name. Just introduce yourself first to the person whose name you forgot. "I'm sorry. I know we've met, but I don't remember your name. I'm Joe Green and this is my friend Tim Short."

NEVER:

✦ Look at the ground or away when you are being introduced to someone.

✦ Refuse to shake a hand extended in greeting.

✦ Crunch someone's hand in a bone-crushing grip or offer your hand as if it's a wet dishrag—a moderately firm grip is best.

✦ Skip the introduction because you've forgotten someone's name.

When You're on Your Own

Once in a while you will find yourself in a situation where you have to introduce yourself. It is really quite simple. Approach the person with a smile, an extended right hand, and a "Hi, my name is Jill Chambers. I just moved in next door." The other person should respond by shaking your hand and telling you his or her name. "Hi, Jill, I'm Charlie. Glad to meet you. Where did you move here from?"

Sticky Situations

PICTURE THIS: You are watching the NBA final playoff game. The score is tied; there is one minute left. Your mother arrives, having just picked up her friend whom you've never met. What do you do?

You should stand up, welcome your mother's friend with a smile and a handshake. Then explain that it is the last few plays of a very close championship game and ask your mom and her friend if they mind if you finish watching the game. You could even invite them to watch with you. They might enjoy it, too.

PICTURE THIS: You are in the inside seat of a booth in a restaurant, your teacher comes into the restaurant, and when he sees you, he comes over to introduce his wife. You can't really stand up. What do you do?

You make the effort as if to stand, reach over the table to shake hands, and greet your teacher and his wife. Do look them in the eye and smile. Extra points . . . do introduce the others at your table. "Mr. and Mrs. James, this is my mom and dad, Pat and Bill Smith."

PICTURE THIS: You've just taken a mouthful of food when your friend comes by and introduces his cousin who is visiting. What do you do?

Keep your mouth closed, point to it or indicate in some way that your mouth is full, chew and swallow as quickly as you safely can, and then say, "Hi, Jim, nice to meet you!" Stand up, too, if you're able to get up from the table easily.

PICTURE THIS: You are leaving school, you have a stack of books on one arm and an open soda in the other. Your teacher is standing at the doorway with the new principal. Your teacher introduces you to her and she extends her hand to shake. What do you do?

You say, "Hello, Mrs. Principal, it's good to meet you. Sorry I can't shake hands. My hands are kind of full."

TECHNO-MANNERS

You are sitting in the food court at the mall. A phone starts ringing. Everybody checks his or her backpack or bag to see if it's his or hers. At one table someone's pager beeps. At another, two young kids are fighting over a Game Boy. You try to call your mother, but the line is busy, which means someone at home is on the Internet—probably your sister visiting her favorite chat room. Ten years ago, this situation wouldn't have been possible. Now, to go along with the many new technological inventions, new manners have also been invented.

All these new gadgets are great to use, but they also can annoy people around us. In general, any time your use of a techno-device is going to disturb other people, turn it off or move to a place where it won't be a problem. In addition, here are some other "new" manners to help you:

◆ **Share with others** if it's a game. Offer your friend a turn with the controls. Alternate games. Ask for suggestions for strategies.

✦ **When you are working at a computer with others, make sure they can see the screen.** Offer someone else a chance at the keyboard. Don't hog it.

✦ **Don't use any new technologies while you are involved in another activity.** Don't play with your Game Boy when you're at your brother's concert. Don't have a long conversation on your cell phone while you're at a game. Turn off your pager in church.

✦ **Follow the rules** already in place wherever you are: school, restaurant, movies, church, etc.

ONLINE ETIQUETTE
(O.L.E!!!)

CHAT ETIQUETTE AND MESSAGE-BOARD MANNERS

Message boards and chat rooms are a great way to share ideas with kids all across the country. But it's no different than any time you get together with other kids—there are rules of behavior that make it a better event for everyone. Here are eight tips for safe, fun visits to chat rooms and message boards:

1. **Never, ever, for any reason share personal information**, such as your real name, address or phone number, age, or sex. If anyone in the chat room asks you for that information, just log off!

2. If the chat room is specific for a certain topic, **talk only about that topic**, not about something else.

3. **Keep your questions and answers short.** Don't tie up a whole page with a long, wordy answer.

4. **Use good language.** Bad language is bad manners in any situation. The fact that no one knows you is no excuse.

PASSWORD PROTECTION
O.L.E.

NEVER, NO WAY, NEVER give your password to anyone—even to your very best friend!

---

5. **Be nice!** The old expression "You catch more flies with honey than with vinegar" applies to chat rooms and message boards, too. And if someone is being mean and nasty to you, don't be mean and nasty back; just log off.

6. **Don't use all CAPS!** It's just the same as shouting and just as rude.

7. **"Listen"**—there may be some great ideas out there. Just as in a face-to-face conversation, you may learn something if you take the time to listen by paying attention to what the other people are writing.

8. **Let the others in the chat room know** when you arrive and when you leave. It is good manners to say "hello" and "good-bye" in any setting.

Remember, if you are bullied or mistreated in any way, you have no social obligation to stay. Online time is meant to be good time. If it's not, simply move on. There's a lot to do, things to learn, and people to meet on the Internet. It is your choice to log on and your choice to log off. Make the choice that's right for you!

Message boards and chat rooms are a great way to share ideas with kids all across the country.

E-LETTERS, E-NOTES, E-CARDS, E-MAIL

E-mail makes communicating easier than ever. You can write a letter to your friend—no stamp necessary—and have it delivered instantly! Websites offer e-postcards. There are e-greeting cards available on the Internet and with software programs. Just as with other types of communication, a whole set of manners has evolved to help us all be considerate and respectful as e-mail races back and forth from computer to computer.

ALWAYS:

+ Check over what you've written before pushing the send button. Sending an e-mail is like dropping a letter in the mail slot—you can't get it back.

+ Take care not to write something that you wouldn't want the world to see. It's very easy for someone to forward that note or cut and paste it into a message of his own.

+ Respect confidentiality. Don't forward a message someone has sent you in confidence.

+ Use the subject line. This lets the person you are e-mailing know that your message isn't spam.

+ Use "reply all" with care. You may not really want everybody on the list to see your reply.

+ Respond as promptly as possible. Let the sender know you got her message, and if you don't have time at the moment, you'll write more later.

NEVER:

+ Open strange mail. If it is not from an address you know, delete it immediately!

◆ Write in caps. Not only is it considered shouting, it is very hard to read.

◆ Send attachments unless you *know* the person you are sending them to has the software needed to open them.

◆ Write a message you may regret sending. If you are mad about something, wait until you're not feeling so emotional before writing about it. That way you won't have anything to regret.

The basic guidelines for writing a letter apply to e-mail correspondence also. Greet the person, think about your content, check spelling and grammar, and use an appropriate closing. (There is no need to date the note, as it is part of the automatic heading of your e-mail.) Just because e-mail is quick and easy to use, there is no need to be lazy about regular letter-writing manners.

FAMILY AND FRIENDS

Unless you are alone in your room using a computer game on your own line, your use of the new technology will have an affect on someone else. Even if you can't see your mother while she is in the kitchen, you need to be considerate of her. Before you tie up the phone with an extended computer chat with your buddies, be sure she doesn't need the phone. If the cordless phone is under the covers in your bedroom, no one else in the family can use it (and the batteries will run out while someone is on an important call). If your good friend is visiting and you spend the whole time on your hand-held computer game, she may not come back.

Techno-manners haven't all been set. Some new technology that you haven't even thought of will be in your home tomorrow. There may not be a rule to guide you in its use. When that's the case, it will be up to you to decide what to do. Think about the other person involved. How will your actions affect him? If you decide how to act based on respect, consideration, and kindness, your actions will always be good ones.

A QUESTION *for* PEGGY & CINDY

QUESTION: *My uncle sent me a great CD for my birthday. Can I send my thank-you note by e-mail?*

ANSWER: *Even though e-mail is easier, the nicest way to thank your uncle is with a snail-mail thank-you note. If you know he checks his e-mail regularly, send a quick e-mail thanks to let him know the CD arrived. Then, once you've had a chance to listen to it, take a few moments to write him a thank-you note. After all, he took the time to pick out the CD, wrap it, and send it to you by mail. The e-mail note will let him know it got there; the thank-you note will show your appreciation.*

CHAPTER TWO

AT HOME
THE FAMILY ZONE

*Love, care, consideration, and kindness are four
essential ingredients of a happy family. However, there is
one more — respect.*

Your friend Jennie lives with her mother, stepfather, two brothers, and a stepsister. Your friend Mack lives with his grandparents. Lillie lives with her mother, father, and sister. You live with your mother and brother. Families come in all shapes and sizes. They all share joys and sorrows, sometimes in very close quarters.

Etiquette is important to building strong family relationships. When you get home, you don't leave respect, honesty, and consideration at the door. If you use good manners with one another, you will strengthen family ties and make your time with your family that much better. The following are some of the basics:

Talk to each other: Do you think your parents are "out of it"? Maybe that's because you leave them out. What about your sister or brother? Clue them in to what's going on in your life and show some interest in what's going on in theirs. Talk to one another! You can often tell when something's wrong. Say something like "You've seemed really down these past few days. Is there anything I can do to help?" Even if there isn't, your family will know you noticed and that you care enough to offer.

Respect privacy: Do you want people barging into your room without knocking, reading your personal journal, or opening your mail before you get home? Probably not. Your family members don't want you doing those things either. If you're not sure whether something is an invasion of privacy or not, just ask yourself how you would feel if someone else did it to you.

Respect possessions: Your stepbrother just bought a new CD. It has a song you really want to hear. He's away for the weekend. The CD is in the rack in his room. You know he won't mind if you just listen to it once. . . . Maybe it works out just fine. You listen, you return it, and all is okay. But what if the CD gets scratched? It may just be a little bump in your relationship. But little bumps can add up to big problems. Make sure you do your part to create a home where everyone respects one another's possessions.

Sharing spaces: Every house has shared space—the kitchen, the living room, the family room, the dining room, or the bathroom. In shared spaces you must balance your personal styles—neat or messy; simple or cluttered—or you will be at one another's throats every day.

And you *must* share the work to keep the spaces livable. This includes picking up, cleaning, and taking your own things back to your room. Sharing space means more than just the physical space—consider televisions, radios, electronic games, computers, and disc players. Sharing space means volume and channel controls, too.

Bathrooms may be the hardest to share. They are private places that are

BATHROOM WARS

You and your sisters share a bathroom. It's 6:30 A.M. Your older sister is in the bathroom. Twenty minutes later she's still there. Finally, it's your turn. Well, if she can take a half hour, so can you. Now your younger sister only has ten minutes or she'll miss the bus. She races out without cleaning the sink, putting the toothpaste cap back, or picking up her wet towel. Your older sister is the first in the bathroom after school. She's not going to clean her sister's mess in the sink and her towel is added to the pile. Your turn—and your choice. Does this bathroom war go on? If not, how can you achieve "bathroom peace?"

often used by two or more people. Cleaning up after someone else's personal mess is gross, so always clean up after yourself. Wash out your own bathtub ring, clean up the spilled toothpaste, wipe off the toilet seat, pick up your used towels, and put your dirty clothes in the hamper. And, if you are a guy, *always* put the toilet seat down when you're done.

Fighting fairly: Even in the best of relationships there are disagreements and fights. Nobody agrees about everything all the time! "Fighting fairly" really means talking to each other, even when you are angry. Sulking and not talking to each other will only make things worse. Yelling, name calling, and swearing add fuel to the fire. There's a better way—talk it out. Here's how:

✦ **Take some time to cool off!** Trying to talk when tempers are flaring usually doesn't work.

- ✦ **Talk calmly.**
- ✦ **Listen** to what the other person has to say.
- ✦ **Let the other person know** what's bothering you.
- ✦ **Try to work out a compromise** that satisfies both of you.
- ✦ **If necessary, ask another family member** for help. This may be a time when your mother or father can help you. Sometimes another view is all you need to find a solution that works for all.

Jealousy—the green-eyed monster: Jealousy is called the green-eyed monster for a reason. It's a monstrous emotion and can wreck the best relationships. Sometimes it seems as if your father pays more attention to your stepsister, your brother has the better room, your sister is prettier, and everyone loves the baby more. You begin to feel resentful and even angry. Watch out! What you are feeling is jealousy. It takes self-confidence and courage to fight jealousy, but if you use your common sense and really look at yourself and your role in the family, you can overcome this destructive emotion. Sometimes you can't do it alone. Try sharing your feelings with another family member. Together you can overcome the green-eyed monster.

RESPECT—THE GLUE THAT HOLDS US TOGETHER

Love, care, consideration, and kindness are four essential ingredients of a happy family. However, there is one more—respect. You should practice the following tips for showing respect until you naturally use them in good times and in bad:

- ✦ **Introduce your friends** to family members when you bring them to the house.
- ✦ **Call family members by the name** they would like you to use—

avoid nicknames that you know they hate.

+ **Don't borrow** things without asking.

+ **Respect** others' privacy.

+ **Don't share personal information** about family members with your friends unless they've given the okay.

+ **Let others know when your plans change**, especially if it means they will need to change theirs.

+ **Let others know if you'll be late** for something.

+ **Participate in family activities** with a positive attitude.

+ **Don't wait to be told or asked** to do things that are already on your list of responsibilities.

+ Sometimes, it's really nice to **help out**, even if something is not on your "to do" list.

> *If you're not sure whether something is an invasion of privacy or not, just ask yourself how you would feel if someone else did it to you.*

A QUESTION *for* PEGGY & CINDY

QUESTION: *Why does it seem like we have different manners for "at home" than we do for when we go out?*

ANSWER: *Home is the place where we can relax and be more informal with one another. We don't need to stand and shake hands each time someone walks in the room. We don't have to wear a coat and tie to dinner. But, no matter how informal or relaxed we are, we don't leave our manners behind when we come home. Respect, consideration, and honesty are essential everywhere, including home!*

THE CHALLENGE OF CHANGE

DIVORCE

Sometimes things don't go the way you've planned them. Anger, resentment, sadness, grief, and a sense of loss are all unhappy emotions that often accompany divorce. Even though you didn't ask for any of them, you do have to deal with them. They are a part of the change divorce has brought to your family.

While many things may seem out of your control, you *can* control how you act by using good manners as you meet the challenges these changes bring to you. The following basic manners that relate specifically to divorce may help you with some awkward situations:

✦ If both your parents attend a school function, **spend time with each of them**. Introduce them both to teachers and friends they haven't met.

✦ **Keep family business personal.** You may talk with your closest friends about how you're feeling and what's happening in your life, but they don't need to hear about your parents' private business.

✦ Even if you're feeling angry at one or both of your parents, be sure to **keep talking to them**, even if only about unimportant, everyday things. By keeping up basic daily conversations, the lines of communication will be open when you're ready to talk about more emotional issues.

✦ Keep in mind that everyone is feeling the effects of change—your brothers, sisters, and grandparents, too. **Don't forget the basics** such as "please" and "thank you" when you're with them, too.

A QUESTION *for* PEGGY & CINDY

QUESTION: *My parents were divorced this year. My birthday is coming up next month. We always opened family presents in the morning and had our birthday party with friends and other family members in the afternoon or evening. Now I don't know what we'll do. Should I ask my parents to celebrate the way we always did? After all, it is my birthday.*

ANSWER: *Even if your parents agree to your request, it will never be the way it was. With a divorce there will be many changes in your family traditions. It will take time to build new traditions that will work for the way your family is now. This first birthday will be the hardest. But with each birthday you celebrate, you will start new traditions that will become familiar and comfortable. Maybe your parents will be able to get together for a celebration; maybe not. The important thing is for you to talk with each of them and to work out enjoyable activities that celebrate your birthday—a special day for sure!*

REMARRIAGE

Just as you are getting used to the changes brought by divorce, you may face altogether new changes. There may be a remarriage for one or both of your parents. Changes can include a new stepfamily, new houses, a move to another town or school, or different living arrangements. One of the keys for moving forward with your life is to do what you can to make this change successful. Use your best manners to get off on the right foot with your new stepparent:

✦ **Get to know him or her.** Use all your conversation skills and include him or her in your conversations.

✦ If there's a wedding ceremony, **ask if you could take part** in the planning. If you're to be in the wedding, find out what you'll be expected to do. Will you be an attendant? Will you have a special role? Where will you sit? The more you know about what to expect, the more you'll be able to enjoy the ceremony.

✦ **Take time to talk to both your parents** about the changes that this marriage will bring. If you show interest, your parents will be more likely to include you in the planning and discussions. If you don't want to talk about things, just say so. "You know, I still really have a hard time talking about this stuff. Whatever you plan will be good by me."

✦ **Tone and attitude are as important** as what you say. Even if you are not happy about the new arrangement, you cannot change it. The only thing you control is your own reactions.

✦ A remarriage means the establishment of a new family unit. It will be different from the one you're used to. Rather than living in a world of comparisons, **try to appreciate the new things** offered by your new family.

✦ **Maybe you'll have stepsiblings.** Make an effort to get to know them. They're probably working hard, too, to get used to their new life. Try to be open-minded about the way they do things, and about things they like. Find some things you can enjoy doing together.

✦ **Your other parent will be feeling some difficult emotions** at this time. Some special kindnesses from you may smooth the way. Offer to do something special for him or her, even something as simple as saying, "I'm getting a soda. Can I get one for you, too?" You could also offer to do something together. "Hey, Mom, I've done my homework. Want to take a bike ride?"

Whether the family change you face is divorce or remarriage, the following may help out:

ALWAYS:

- ✦ Be honest about what you are feeling.
- ✦ Treat all family members with respect.
- ✦ Offer to help out.
- ✦ Keep lines of communication open.
- ✦ Keep up with your responsibilities, including chores and schoolwork.

NEVER:

- ✦ Gossip about what's going on in your family life.
- ✦ Lash out at others with mean, negative talk.
- ✦ Make threats you may not want to keep ("I'm never going to visit Dad in that house").
- ✦ Isolate yourself from family and friends who may be trying to offer you support.

MEALTIME MANNERS MATTER

Mealtime manners do matter. Many get-togethers with family and friends are for a meal. How we act and what we say sets the stage for either a great time or an embarrassment. What if you start eating as soon as you sit down and then discover the family you are visiting says grace before eating? What can you do if you get food caught in your teeth? What should you do if you drink from your neighbor's glass? Table manners give us guidelines for all these predicaments and more.

THE FUNDAMENTALS

If you follow these guidelines, you can avoid embarrassing moments and enjoy your meal without nervousness:

- ✦ **Arrive at the table with clean hands** and face.
- ✦ **Place your napkin** on your lap right off.
- ✦ **Start eating when given the okay by your host,** or when everyone else does.
- ✦ **Sit up straight** and stay seated.
- ✦ **Keep your elbows off** the table while eating.
- ✦ **Chew** with your mouth closed.
- ✦ **Don't talk with food in your mouth.** If you have to wait until you've swallowed before answering a question, that's fine.
- ✦ **Don't criticize** the food.
- ✦ **Ask for food to be passed**; say "Please," and don't reach.
- ✦ **Talk with everyone** at the table.
- ✦ **Don't make rude noises** such as burping or snorting.
- ✦ **Ask to be excused** when finished.
- ✦ **Thank the person** who prepared the meal.
- ✦ **Offer to help** clear the table.

TABLE SETTINGS—THE NOT-SO-SECRET CODE

Table settings send a message about what kind of meal you are going to have. One quick glance and you know if you're having soup, whether salad will be served before or after the main course, if a hot beverage will be served, and if the adults at the table will be having wine. Everyone at the table knows what to expect. Will it be an informal family meal or a very formal dinner? Just one look at the table and you'll know!

Family Meal

The standard family place setting is typically used at everyday meals. A fork, knife, spoon, napkin, plate, and a glass are all you need.

Informal Three-Course Dinner

The informal three-course dinner is set for all the courses served during dinner, so there will be more utensils than at the simple family meal. You are more likely to see this setting at fine restaurants and parties or receptions where a sit-down meal is served. Some of the additional pieces and their places in the setting are:

✦ **Salad fork:** The location of the salad fork tells you when your salad will be served. If it is to the left of the large dinner fork, your salad will be served before the main course. If it is to the right, your salad will be served after the main course.

✦ **Soupspoon** is at the far right of the place setting.

✦ **Dessert spoon** goes to the left of the soupspoon, next to the knife (or horizontally above the plate).

✦ **Salad plate** goes to the left of the forks.

✦ **Butter plate and butter knife** (laid across the plate) are above the forks.

✦ **Glasses** are set above and slightly to the right of the dinner plate. The first one on the left is the water glass. Next comes your other glass (milk, juice, soda, iced tea). Wine glasses (if the adults are having wine) go to the right of the water glass.

✦ **Coffee cup and saucer** are above and slightly to the right of the knife, with the coffee spoon resting on the right side of the saucer.

> ## HOW DO I EAT MY SOUP?
>
> *In order to avoid sloshing or scooping soup into your lap, spoon the soup from the edge nearest you to the edge away from you. It's okay to gently tilt the bowl to get that last drop. Just tip your bowl away from you for the same reason. Then sip—don't slurp!—the soup from the side of your soupspoon. When you're finished, leave the spoon on the plate under the soup bowl instead of in the bowl.*

Formal Dinner

Table settings get more complicated as the dinners get more formal. That's because at a formal dinner there are more courses, and for each course there are more utensils and plates. At a very formal dinner you may have as many as three (sometimes even four) forks, two spoons, three knives, and four glasses. Which do you use first? There is an easy rule to follow. Whether it's a formal dinner out or supper at home in the kitchen, start from the outside and work your way in with each course.

The easiest thing to do is to watch everyone around you—especially the adults you're with.

A QUESTION *for* PEGGY & CINDY

QUESTION: *I am going to a very formal dinner at my cousin's wedding reception. I don't think I can remember all the extra table manners that go with a formal dinner. What do I do?*

ANSWER: *The easiest thing to do is to watch everyone around you—especially the adults you're with. Don't eat anything until they do. You can check out which fork they use, how they eat certain foods, and where they put their utensils when they're done.*

STICKY SITUATIONS

You bite on something that you know is NOT food.

Not a problem! Remove the item from your mouth by quietly placing it back on your fork and then putting it on the edge of your plate. If you see something in your food, remove it without comment and place it on the edge of your plate. In a restaurant, quietly tell your server about the problem and ask for a new portion.

You spill your glass of juice. It is running across the table toward your friend's lap.

Warn your friend! Try to clean up the juice with your napkin as quickly as possible. Get the juice that's running toward your friend first! Use some paper towels or a sponge if you need it. If the spill lands on someone—especially if it's hot—take care of the person first and worry about the mess later. If it was something solid (like you knocked all the peas off

HOW DO I EAT IT?

Spoon or pour ketchup for French fries onto your plate and then dip the fries individually. French fries are considered a finger food, and you may use either your fingers or your fork to eat them. However, if they are drenched in gravy or are served with foods you eat with a fork (such as a steak), use your fork for the fries, too.

your plate), pick them up with a spoon and put them back on the edge of your plate.

You feel a sneeze coming on—fast! Or you swallow wrong and you are coughing like crazy!

Cover your mouth with a handkerchief, your napkin, or your hand. If the sneezing or coughing continues, excuse yourself—assuring the others that you are okay. You should also leave the table to blow your nose. Find a bathroom, get a sip of water, blow your nose, and wash your hands before returning to the table.

You have a piece of food stuck in your teeth or braces. You tried getting it off with your tongue, but it's still there.

Just excuse yourself and go to the restroom to remove it. Don't use toothpicks, floss, or your fingers at the table.

The Trouble with Bubbles—or Some Thoughts About Drinking

Whether it's milk, juice, soda, or water, there is a temptation to play with your beverage—especially when it is served with a straw. Blowing bubbles, gargling, gulping, and spitting can be somewhat amusing, but they are not okay while eating a meal at the table under any circumstances. When drinking . . .

ALWAYS:

- ✦ Drink slowly, taking no more than one or two swallows at a time.
- ✦ Swallow the beverage immediately.
- ✦ Chew and swallow food before taking a drink.
- ✦ Take small sips from a glass that is too full until you've had enough to allow careful drinking.

NEVER:

✦ Swish, slosh, gurgle, or gargle your beverage.

✦ Blow bubbles in your milk (or any other beverage).

✦ Chug the whole glassful at one time.

✦ Upend or lick at the glass to get the last drop.

A FEW WORDS ABOUT WORDS AT THE TABLE

HOW DO I USE IT?

If you have a lemon wedge for flavoring tea or other beverages, squeeze it directly over the drink. Then you can either drop the wedge into your glass or cup, or put it on the side of your plate. If you choose to squeeze the lemon, it is considerate to shield it with your other hand to prevent it from squirting others at the table.

Mealtime is about more than just eating. Imagine a meal where everyone comes in, sits down, eats the food, gets up, clears the table, and goes back to what he or she was doing without saying a word. Or, think about a meal where everyone is talking, listening, laughing, or even having a serious talk about things that are going on in school. Which dinner would you rather go to?

Good mealtime manners include good conversation. Here are some tips for talking at the table:

✦ **Look at the person you're speaking with;** remember to talk to people on both sides of you.

✦ **Pay attention** (eye contact is good!), and show interest in what people are saying. Make comments and answer their questions.

✦ **Don't interrupt.**

✦ **Speak clearly** when it's your turn.

✦ **Don't talk with your mouth full.**

✦ **Include everyone** at the table.

✦ **Avoid loud talking** and gross topics.

✦ **Say something good** about the food when you can; don't criticize the food (forget about saying, "It's yucky!").

✦ **Remember to thank** whoever prepared (or bought if you're at a restaurant) the meal.

TALK, TALK, TALK

You've been at school with your friends all day, you went to baseball practice together after school, but now you just have to call your friend to talk about all the things you forgot to say earlier. The telephone is an

CALL-WAITING— A BUILT-IN INTERRUPTION

A basic rule of etiquette is not to interrupt; yet call-waiting is a built-in interruption. How rude! So . . . you're on the phone with a friend and call waiting beeps. What do you do?

✦ *If the signal can be heard by both of you, just say, "There's a call waiting. I just need to check who it is. I'll be right back." If your friend can't hear the tone, wait until he ends his sentence and then interrupt and say that you have a call on the other line that you have to check.*

✦ *If the call is for you, just say you're on the line and you'll call right back. Go back to your first friend, finish your conversation, and then call your other friend back—soon.*

✦ *If the call is for your mother, ask the person to hold while you get her. Then go back to your friend, tell him there is a call for your mother and you'll call him back. Next, quickly get your mom. Be sure to ask her to let you know when she's done so you can call your friend back.*

✦ *Do NOT keep the first caller waiting while you chat with the call-waiting caller.*

amazing tool! And a shared tool, too. Your parents, brothers, and sisters all want to use it, too, and people outside the house want to use it to contact them. Each family has to determine guidelines that will make sure that the phone is a useful tool for all, not the object of fights and disagreements.

Manners help us to use the telephone the right way. The following basic guidelines may help prevent confusion:

+ **Answer the phone with a nice greeting**—"Hello" instead of just "Yeah."

+ **If the call is for someone else, keep it simple:**

  + "Just a minute, I'll get her." Or, if you know the caller, "Oh, hi Mrs. Blake. I'll get her."

  + Gently put down the phone—without dropping it.

  + Go get the person the call is for; don't stand beside the phone and yell.

  + If you know who it is, tell the person. "Mom, it's Mrs. Blake for you."

+ If the person the caller wants to speak to isn't there, **offer to take a message**. "Mary's not here right now; can I take a message?" (See taking and leaving messages on page 55.)

+ **When you call others, say "Hello,"** identify yourself, and ask for the person you want to speak to. If you know the person who answers, add his or her name to your greeting. "Hi, Mark. This is Carrie Brooks. Could I please speak to Jenny?" Avoid slangy grunts such as, "Hey—Jenny there?"

+ **If you have to sneeze or cough**, move the mouthpiece away from you. To the other person, it may sound like a freight train coming through the phone.

SAFE PHONE ANSWERING

Don't give your name when you answer the phone. If it's a wrong number, just say so without giving out your number. "You must have the wrong number."

What to do if a stranger calls: Rather than telling a stranger you are home alone, you can say, "Mom's busy right now. Can I take a message?"

If a caller starts saying mean or inappropriate things, hang up immediately. Then call your parents or tell whoever's in charge about the call.

If you have an answering machine, use it to screen calls. When the phone rings, let the answering machine take the call and pick up the phone only if you know the caller.

Your Voice Is All the Other Person Can "See"

When you talk on a phone, your voice is the only clue the other person has as he or she tries to "see" you. Here are some tips so you can help the person see the best in you:

+ **Don't mumble.** Speak clearly so the other person understands what you are saying.

+ **Smile!** Even if they can't see you, they can tell the difference between a "Hi" with a smile and a "Yeah, what do you want?" which can't be said with a smile.

+ **Use inflection.** If you talk in a monotone, you will sound uninteresting.

+ **Don't chew gum**, drink, or eat. Enough said!

Taking and Leaving Messages

ALWAYS:

   ◆ Write the name of the caller, his or her phone number (if needed), date, time, and message.

   ◆ Write legibly and leave the message someplace where it will be seen by the person it's for.

   ◆ Answering machine: If you listen to the messages, let others know if there are messages for them.

   ◆ Erase your own messages once you've heard them.

NEVER:

   ◆ Assume you will "remember" the message. Always write it down.

   ◆ Give out detailed information. "Oh, hi, Bob. Mary's out with Ted right now." Mary may not want Bob to know she is out with Ted. Instead say, "Mary's not here right now. May I take a message?"

   ◆ Erase other people's messages from the answering machine.

FAMILY DECISIONS

Many families establish their own rules about phones and phone use. Things to take into consideration: Family size, finances (phone bills add up!), age, and level of responsibility of phone users. Things not to be considered: what your friend's family does. Some of these decisions include:

- **One line** or two.
- **Length of calls:** If you don't have call-waiting or caller ID, the considerate thing is to limit calls to thirty minutes.
- **Calling times:** A good guide is no earlier than 9:00 in the morning and no later than 9:00 at night. Or, you might call before or after the nine-to-nine time frame if you know a friend's family does not mind.
- **Long-distance calls:** Establish a time limit, and whether or not you have to ask permission first.
- **Cell phones:** If you have or use one, all the guidelines for phone use in this chapter apply. See pages 107–8 for guidelines for use of cell phones in public.

CHAPTER THREE

AT SCHOOL
GOOD MORNING, MRS. JONES

Follow the guidelines and classroom rules, do your work to the best of your ability, and use good manners. Consider this as good practice for the day that may come when you have a boss you don't like.

School is the first place where manners really begin to work for you. Most of your day in school is spent in the classroom. Your teacher, the other students, and you are like a cross between a job and a family. One way to get others to respect you is to show respect for them. There are eight important manners for the classroom that help make it a respectful place for everyone:

1. **Make an effort to greet everyone** with, at least, a "Good morning" and a smile. Adding a comment such as "How was your game yesterday?" or "Mrs. Jones, that chapter we read last night was hard!" makes others feel included and lets them know you are a friendly person.

2. **Call teachers and any other adults in the classroom by the name and title they prefer.** Some teachers prefer to be called by their first names,

but unless they specifically ask you to do that, call them by their correct name and title.

3. **Call your friends by the names they prefer.** Nicknames may seem fun, but sometimes they can be very hurtful. We know about a class where all the kids called a boy "Meatball." We asked another student if he thought it bothered him. "Oh no, he doesn't mind. He thinks it's really funny." It was years later before they discovered how much he hated that nickname.

4. **Follow classroom guidelines** for getting up, walking around, leaving to go to the restroom. Each classroom may be different. The important thing is to respect the rules set up for the room you are in.

5. **Sit up at your desk or table** just the way you do at mealtime. Lying all over your desk as if you're tired or bored is both rude and disrespectful. If you're that tired in class, you need to get more sleep the night before. If you're that bored, you need to make the choice to get more involved.

6. **Keep the area around your desk and locker neat.** What it looks like inside is your problem; what it looks like on the outside becomes everyone's problem.

7. **Chip in to help keep shared spaces neat** and picked up—the sink, the reading area, the computer stations, and the bulletin boards.

8. **Greet others who come into your room.** In some schools the rule is

that students stand when adults enter the room and call them "Sir" or "Ma'am." (In Louisiana it is a state law.) The point is that you show respect by using the greeting that is normal in your school.

RELATIONSHIPS IN THE CLASSROOM

With Other Students

WHAT IF . . . *You are assigned to a class, team, or group for the whole year. None of your good friends are assigned with you. What do you do?*

You could mope around for a year and complain. Or you could choose to make the best of it. Look at it as an opportunity to get to know some other kids in your grade. You may discover that your circle of friends gets bigger. Or you might find you focus more on your schoolwork and visit with your friends at other times during the school day. Class time is not the time for hanging out with friends anyway.

With the Teacher

It's easy to act respectfully to the teachers you like. It's much harder to act respectfully to the ones you don't like—especially if they are not always respectful to you. It's a real challenge—a test of your ability to be a better person. Follow the guidelines and classroom rules, do your work to the best

NOT DOING THEIR SHARE?

Four of you are assigned to do a team science project. You and one team member are doing all the work. The other two are just gliding on your effort. What to do?

It's time to call a team meeting. Make a list of all the work to be done (including work you are already doing). As a group, make decisions about who will do what, without making a big deal about who's not doing what. *The others may respond better if this is a team effort. If this doesn't work, you will need to have another team meeting—and this time ask the teacher to join you. She can help out, or at least she'll be aware of what's going on, and you won't be in a position of having to complain about a teammate.*

of your ability, and use good manners. Consider this as good practice for the day that may come when you have a boss you don't like. By using good manners and acting in the ways you know are right, you can be proud of yourself. That will build up your self-respect, and you wind up a winner.

BEYOND THE CLASSROOM

BEFORE AND AFTER SCHOOL, RECESS, AT THE LOCKERS, IN THE HALLS

Schoolwork happens in the classroom. School social life happens outside the classroom—in the halls, at the lockers, before and after school, and during recess. This is where kids find out who's doing what, who's going where with whom, and who likes (or doesn't like) whom. They make plans for the weekend. They compare notes about the latest homework assignment, last Saturday's school dance, the latest CD by your favorite rock group, or yesterday's basketball game. It's also where kids feel included or excluded. School life that takes place outside of the classroom is a very important part of kids' social lives.

While this may feel like unstructured time, there are guidelines that help keep this school social life civil. School rules about bullying, fighting, noise, and fair play give structure to this time. Good manners help us make this time positive.

With Your Friends

CONSIDER THIS: You have a good friend who is always making demands rather than asking. For instance, she's more apt to say "Give me that sweater" than "Please hand me that sweater. Thanks." Which approach do you like better? There is a set of basic manners you can use that will make friendships stronger.

✦ **Use "please" and "thank you"** even with your closest friends.

✦ **Be honest.** Honesty is one of the most important ingredients to good friendships.

✦ **Respect privacy.** Even if you know your friend's combination, don't go in his locker unless he says it's okay.

✦ **Offer to help** when your friend is in a fix.

✦ **Make positive comments.** Give compliments. If you think her new skirt is a great color, say so!

✦ **Be interested** in what she is doing. That means listening to what your friend is saying, and not always talking about yourself.

With Others

School is not a place where kids can hang out with just their own friends. There are others who share this time and space. Sometimes kids get so busy with their friends, they act rudely without even meaning to. Rude behavior is not only hurtful to the other person; it can also hurt the person behaving rudely.

BULLIES
WHAT TO DO

It can be frightening to be the target of a bully. But what can you do? Don't take on the bully yourself. Instead, let your parents know what's going on. Together with them, talk to your teacher or the principal. Describe exactly what is going on. They'll help you know what to do if it happens again. Then your teacher and school administrators can deal with the bully. It is their responsibility to assure your safety at school and help you and your parents deal with the situation. But they can't do it if you don't let them know what's going on.

PICTURE THIS: A group of kids are talking and laughing near the entrance to the school. Just as you walk by they all stop talking and then start again once you have gone in. Or they're whispering, laughing, and pointing your way. Are they talking about you? Or is it the boy walking behind you? Will you ever know? How does it feel?

The next time you are talking and laughing with a group of your friends, give some thought to the others around you. Whispering and pointing are actions that can leave others feeling uncomfortable. These simple things can change the whole picture.

- **Say "Hi"** when someone walks by.
- **Avoid whispering** and pointing.
- **Save very personal conversations for somewhere private** so you don't have to stop talking when others walk by.
- **Open the door** for others with a heavy load.
- **Make space for others** when in a crowded hallway.
- **Smile!**

A QUESTION *for* PEGGY & CINDY

QUESTION: *I'm the new kid in my school. There is a group of kids who play soccer during recess. Is there something I can do to join in without seeming pushy?*

ANSWER: *Sure! Start out by standing back and watching the group. Be open about it. You'll want to see if other kids are joining in and then leaving. Get a sense for how the group works. Then show an interest in the group. If a ball goes* *out of bounds, pick it up and toss it back into the game. And then, unless it is an official league team, ask to join in. As the group breaks up, approach one or two of the kids and say, "Any chance you have room for another player? I really liked playing soccer at my old school." Don't be discouraged if they say the team is full. As you make some friends during other school activities, you will become part of a group. It may not be the first one you approach, but with a little time you'll soon be playing again.*

Another way would be to make an effort to get to know just one of the kids in the group. Then you can ask him to help you join in the game.

Disagreements, Arguments, and Fights

> ### CHOOSING SIDES
>
> *Whether it's for a game at recess or an activities club, kids sometimes have to go through a process of selecting teams. Avoid choosing only your best friends. Think about the talents of the kids in your class. You'll need kids with different skills if your team is to function at its best. It is also a great way to expand your circle of friends. You may discover that the girl who dresses a little differently from you has a great sense of humor and is really fun to be with.*

WHAT IF . . . Your best friend uses your handheld computer game without asking. You feel very angry. But none of your other friends are angry, so they still hang out with the culprit. What can you do?

YOU HAVE A CHOICE:

1. **Hold a grudge,** stay away, don't talk to her or your friends, make new friends.

2. **Yell at her,** call her names, yell at your old friends, go find new friends.

3. **Forget it** and go back to being friends without saying anything.

4. **Ask her to sit and talk**—without your other friends. Tell her how upset you are and why.

YOUR BEST CHOICE: Go for number 4. Why? You'll be taking responsibility for your own feelings. You can say: "When you took my Game Boy without asking, I felt angry because I thought you would have asked." You're in control of your own anger. Don't give her the power to make you angry whenever she chooses. Let her know how you feel about what she did. Make a plan for how you'll both behave in the future (she'll ask when she wants to use your game; you'll let each other know when either of you is angry). And then go on with your friendship. If you make this choice, you won't be letting the disagreement ruin your friendship.

GETTING THERE AND HOME AGAIN

Just getting to school can be a challenge. Some kids have a long walk. Others ride a bus for as much as an hour each way. Some pack into a car with babies, toddlers, and other schoolkids. And some ride bikes, balancing books, lunch boxes, or school projects as they go. No matter how you get to school, there are some key manners that will make getting there and home again fun and safe for everyone.

WALKING TO SCHOOL

CONSIDER THIS: Every morning at 8 A.M. you meet up with four friends for the twenty-minute walk to school. No matter where you live, the manners are simple:

✦ **Cross at corners** or in crosswalks and with the green, or walk light, if there is a stoplight.

✦ **Follow directions** from the crossing guards.

✦ **Don't try to walk and talk** on your cell phone at the same time.

✦ **Do NOT accept rides with strangers** for any reason.

City sidewalks are crowded with business people rushing to work.

✦ **Don't walk five across.** Walk singly or in pairs.

✦ **Keep to the right**, walking in the same direction as the others around you.

✦ **Watch that your backpack** doesn't swing around and hit another walker.

Town sidewalks may not be so crowded, so manners may differ.

✦ **If you walk as a group, give way** if someone comes in the opposite direction.

✦ **Watch for cars** pulling out of driveways.

Rural roads may not have a sidewalk so . . .

✦ **Walk on the left**, so you can see cars coming toward you.

✦ **Keep near the edge** of the road and walk single file when cars are coming.

---

5 TIPS FOR BIKING TO SCHOOL

*S*ome schools and parents allow kids *to travel to and from school on bikes. Here are five tips if you get to school by bike:*

1. **Wear your helmet.** *You can keep it in your locker during the day.*

2. **Be sure you have a basket** *or panniers for carrying your lunch and books.*

3. If you're riding with a friend, **ride single file.**

4. The roads may be especially crowded around the school where buses and cars are arriving to drop off students so **WATCH OUT!**

5. **Park your bike** *in the bike rack and use a lock to secure it during the day.*

CARS AND CARPOOLING

Whether it's just you and your mother or you're in someone else's car with every seat full, you need to mind your car manners.

WHAT IF . . . *You get in the car and you can't get the seat belt fastened?*

YOU WOULD . . . Ask the driver to wait while you buckle up. "Mrs. Bradley, could you please wait a second? I can't get my seat belt buckled."

WHAT IF . . . *You didn't have time for breakfast so you grabbed a banana on your way out?*

YOU WOULD . . . Wait until you get to school to eat it. Some people don't like the smell of certain foods. Also, then you're stuck with a banana peel and nowhere to put it. And some people have strict rules about not eating in their cars.

WHAT IF . . . *It's your mom's turn to drive. You are sitting in the front seat. Your friends in the back are getting louder and fooling around.*

YOU COULD . . . Say, "Come on guys, knock it off. Mom's trying to drive here." They'll feel much better hearing it from you, and she'll really appreciate it.

No matter whose car you're in, when you get to school, be sure to take all your stuff and remember to thank the driver!

RIDING THE BUS

School bus drivers have an awesome responsibility. They drive as many as seventy-two children to and from school every day. Safety is the number one thing on their mind. But they also provide the space where all those kids spend anywhere from a half hour to two hours a day. The atmosphere on the bus has a major impact on how kids feel for the rest of the day. So that is also on the driver's mind.

Kids share in the awesome responsibility. How kids behave affects both the safety and the atmosphere on the bus. Even if the bus driver seems grumpy, try giving a smile and a friendly good morning when you get on.

A thank-you as you get off may pave the way for a better ride the next time. Get on and off quickly. Cars are required to stop for a school bus with lights flashing. If kids are pokey as they move down the aisle, cars are tempted to pass. The bus driver is trying to keep on schedule. When kids follow the rules, everyone is safer; when kids are friendly and polite, the whole atmosphere becomes more pleasant.

There are some clear *always* and *nevers* associated with bus riding.

ALWAYS:

✦Wait for the bus driver's signal before crossing the road getting on or off the bus.

✦ Have your things organized so you can quickly get on or off.

✦ Keep your voices low. A lot of noise can be very distracting for the driver.

✦ Buckle up on buses where seat belts are available.

NEVER:

- ◆ Fight—especially on the bus.
- ◆ Throw things.
- ◆ Bait the driver.
- ◆ Stand or move about the bus when it is moving.

A QUESTION *for* PEGGY & CINDY

QUESTION: *Sometimes at my bus stop some of my friends tease the little kids. I want to say something, but they'll just say I'm being a goody-goody. What should I do?*

ANSWER: *You should say something. "Hey, Tommy—let them alone." And then talk about something else. "Anyway, did you see that game last night?" Don't lecture. Just turn the conversation to something less hurtful. Talk about homework, yesterday's practice, or your upcoming trip this weekend—anything to turn the attention from teasing. You'll be glad you did.*

EATING ON THE RUN

School lunch can be crazy. You may be scheduled at 11:00 and have fifteen minutes to eat, but your best friend may have lunch at 12:30 and have forty-five minutes to eat. Some people are rushing just to get anything to eat at all. Others don't have any of their friends scheduled with them and have to sit with people they don't know. It's a recipe for frayed nerves and short tempers.

CONSIDERATION—

MAKING MRS. P.'S DAY BETTER

PICTURE THIS: *Mrs. P. works in a cafeteria line. Her job is to serve a scoop of mashed potatoes to each of four hundred students in two hours. As the kids come through the line, some say, "Hi, Mrs. P. How's it going?" Others say, "Thanks" or "No, thanks." But some say, "This stuff is really gross!" What a difference a few words can make!*

*   **Consideration** means thinking about the other person. You do something just to make his or her situation a little better. Working in a cafeteria line is not easy. Just by the way you pass through that line, you can make a difference in the server's day. You won't get a good grade for it. No one will pay you. No one else will ever know. But Mrs. P. will. And you will, too.*

SOME BASICS NEVER CHANGE

Manners have changed to go with this rushed setting. But no matter how they've changed, how fast you have to eat, how crowded the table is, or who is sitting at the table, manners are just as important in the school cafeteria as they are at home or in a fine restaurant.

ALWAYS:

✦ Say "Please," "Thank you," and "Excuse me" to the staff who are serving food in the lunch line and the kids you sit with at the table.

✦ Pick up after yourself. Clean up any spills, pick up paper wrappers, napkins, and cups, and clear your tray.

✦ Make room for the next group coming in. Even if you still have time when you're done eating, leave the cafeteria and do your socializing in the recess area.

NEVER:

+ Chew with your mouth open. That's just as gross in the cafeteria as it is anywhere else.

+ Talk with your mouth full. No one can understand you, and you could choke.

+ Throw your food, play with it, or blow bubbles and slurp your drink.

+ Burp out loud or make other rude noises at the table.

There are some special manners that help keep school lunchtimes as civil as possible. If everyone follows these guidelines, lunch can still be an opportunity to socialize with friends as you eat a quick lunch. If kids ignore these guidelines, the lunchroom becomes a disaster zone, the school might put rigid rules in place, and lunch would become a simple refueling stop with no opportunity to talk with friends.

SIX TIPS TO PREVENT LUNCHROOM MAYHEM:

1. **Do follow the directions of the adult in charge** at all times, even if she is not seated at your table.

2. **Don't push, shove, or engage in rough play** of any kind in the lunch lines.

3. **Do hold your food tray with two hands,** and don't touch other kids' trays or food.

4. **Don't ask for someone else's food.** And don't offer your food to others at the table.

5. **Don't make comments about other kids' meals** or eating styles. Just because a classmate follows a special diet or brings lunch from home while others buy theirs is no excuse for rude or teasing remarks.

6. **Don't exclude others from your table** if you have an empty seat.

When You Have Time

If you see someone sitting alone during lunch day after day, try joining her, or invite her to join your group for lunch. She may eat alone because she is rushed and her friends eat at a different time, or she may say, "Thanks, but I'm headed right off to class." On the other hand, she may be lonely. While this simple kindness may not be noticed by anyone else, it could make a difference in her day, and perhaps, surprisingly, it might make a difference in yours.

Other Adults in Your School

There are many adults in schools besides the teachers and principal. Because they are not in positions of authority or responsible for giving grades, some kids ignore them. It takes secretaries, janitors, aides, nurses, librarians, cooks, and cafeteria workers to make a school work. It is just as important to be polite to them as to the teacher and the principal. You can't turn manners on and off. So the next time you pass the janitor in the lunchroom, show some respect; give him the same greeting you would give your teacher.

CHAPTER FOUR

AT PLAY
PARTY TIME!

"You don't have to wait for your birthday to have a party."

Parties are the ultimate social event. The whole purpose of a party is to get together with your friends for a fun time. Sometimes you have a special theme, or you may be celebrating an event, or you may want to have friends over for fun. No matter what the occasion, there are certain things you can do to be sure the party is the best ever and everybody has a great time.

So, let's begin at the beginning!

PLANNING

Plan, plan, plan! The more you settle beforehand, the better your party will be. Certain things have to be decided:

- ✦ **When and where**, including date, time of day, and address.
- ✦ **Theme** (if there will be one).
- ✦ **Number of guests** and who you will invite—all girls, all boys, or mixed.
- ✦ **Will there be a meal?** Snacks? Beverages? If so, what?

◆ **What activities** will there be?

This is a great time to team up with your mom or dad. Like it or not, you'll need your parents' cooperation and involvement to have your party, so involve them right away. That way they'll feel as if they're a part of the planning, and you'll have turned a potential argument into an enjoyable event for everyone.

Guest List

Who will be invited? One of the hardest things to do when having a party is deciding on the guest list. You don't want to leave people out or hurt feelings, but you have to stay within certain numbers, and you want to have people over who you think will get along well. Maybe your soccer buddies won't get along that well with your dance class friends—or, maybe they will. It's often guesswork as to which of your friends would enjoy one another. But it's fun to try "mixing" them up; sometimes the best parties are the ones made up of guests who didn't know one another before. After all, they have you in common. They might also have some interests in common. Putting together a good guest list is the most important thing you do when you give a party. Everything else can be perfect, but if you haven't invited guests who get along or if you've hurt some people's feelings, the party will not be the success you hope for.

Invitations

Are you going to write the invitations or call? Either way there are some important things to consider when you do your invitations.

By phone: Make your invitation in a straightforward manner. "Hi, Macey. I'm having a party next Saturday afternoon, and I hope you can come." Do not start with a question, "What are you doing Saturday afternoon?" You'll put your guest on the spot! That's because if she answers, "Nothing," and

GUEST LIST DILEMMA
MULTIPLE CHOICE

WHAT IF . . . *You are having a party. You want to invite everyone in your class, but there is one girl you really don't like very well and you don't want to invite her.*

WOULD YOU . . .

1. Invite all the others and leave her out?

2. Invite everyone including her?

3. Choose a different grouping of friends for this party so you don't have to leave just one person out?

CORRECT ANSWER: *Either 2 or 3 could work. With 2 you open up to the possibility that she might end up being really fun and a great addition to your party, even if she isn't your favorite person. Three simply suggests you pick a different group so it isn't so obvious you are leaving this one person out. For instance, invite the kids who live right in your neighborhood or who are on your sports team. Or, this time, just invite half your class. You can have another party later when you can invite the others. You should never choose 1. The risk is too great that this one classmate would be really hurt if you invited everyone but her.*

then you invite her, she may feel she has to say yes. What if she really would rather stay home? Other invitation dos and don'ts include:

1. **Be clear about the date,** times, and location of the party.

2. **Give your guest directions** if they don't know the way.

3. **Don't put pressure on** people to say yes.

4. **Do let them know about anything special** they should bring, such as bathing suits, baseball mitts, or CDs.

In writing: Be sure you send out your invitations far enough in advance. Sometimes it takes a few days for mail delivery. If you do have a theme for your party, design an invitation that fits with the theme and be sure to mention it.

1. **Write legibly!**

2. **Say who is giving the party.** If a couple of friends are giving the party together, list all of them alphabetically.

3. **Be clear about the date,** times, and location of the party.

4. **Include a map** if the place is not familiar to everyone you are asking.

5. **Indicate what kind of response** you would like—for a call, put your phone number; a written response, your address; and an e-mail, your e-mail address.

6. **If your written invitations are handed out at school,** make sure that *everyone* in your class—or your group, or team—receives one. Also, make sure your teacher says it's okay to hand out invitations at school.

A QUESTION *for* PEGGY & CINDY

QUESTION: *My mother is planning to be there the whole time. How can I tell her the party is for my friends, not for her?*

ANSWER: *You should discuss this with your mother before the party. If you start by saying that you know she will be at home and coming in and out of the party, it will be easier to ask her not to join in all the activities. Hopefully, she'll understand that you and your friends would be more comfortable without a grown-up there the whole time. Parents should be visibly present when kids are arriving, they should come in and out (maybe serve some food so it doesn't look as if they are hovering), and at the end of the party, they should be around to say good-bye to kids as they leave. They may watch television in another room or be busy in the kitchen during the party, but they should be nearby. If you and your parents talk this out ahead of time, you will find that the party goes much more easily.*

When Your Guests Arrive and Leave

ALWAYS:

◆ Greet each guest with a smile and a hello.

◆ Introduce your guests to your parents and any other family members who are there, if they haven't met before.

◆ Tell your guests where they can put their coats.

◆ Be available to say good-bye when it's time for guests to leave.

◆ Thank each guest for coming.

◆ Let your parents (or the chaperones) know if one of the guests doesn't have a ride.

NEVER:

◆ Ignore guests when they arrive just because you are in a conversation. Simply excuse yourself, go to greet them, and make introductions as needed.

◆ Forget to introduce guests to one another.

◆ Keep a guest waiting when he or she is ready to leave. Instead, break off your conversation by saying, "Excuse me—I need to say good-bye to Margie," and then return to your conversation after the guest leaves.

During the Party

During the party it is your job to be sure everyone is included, is offered beverages and food, and has a chance to participate in activities. (See "Being a Good Host" on page 82.)

◆ If it is a birthday party and you open your gifts during the party, **thank each person for the gift** he or she brought.

◆ If there is food to be served, **make sure everyone has plenty to eat** before you sit down to eat.

◆ If there are planned activities, **describe to everyone all the instructions** and hand out any special materials needed for the activity to each guest.

Most important is to watch what's happening. Is someone being left out? Is someone getting loud and obnoxious? Is one group whispering and giggling and ignoring the others? Is the music too loud? Do people seem bored? Some might be an easy fix; some more difficult. That is the challenge of hosting a party. "Hey, everybody, let's get going with the croquet match" may be all you need to say to get everyone participating. Or you might need to get your parent in to help out if the problem is a guest who misbehaves. Remember, the more you plan ahead and the more activities you have to draw on, the easier it will be for the guests to enjoy themselves—including you.

IDEAS FOR FIVE FUN PARTIES

Everybody enjoys going to a good party. Having parties goes all the way back to first birthdays. Parents pretty much plan those early parties for you. As you get older, you may help with the planning, guest list, and activities for your birthday party (unless it's a surprise). But you probably don't want to limit parties to once a year. You don't have to wait for your birthday to have a party.

Parties can be large or small. A successful party is one where the guests get along well, the activities are fun, and the food is good. The first step is to decide on the type of party. The second step is your parents: clearing the idea with them; making sure the date works for them; figuring out with them how to pay for the party; making sure they can help with any transportation or cooking that needs to happen. The following are party ideas that you might enjoy with your friends.

FOR A SMALL GROUP (FOUR TO SIX GUESTS)

The Classic Slumber Party

Invite four to six friends over. Ask them to arrive in time for supper and to bring sleepwear and their favorite pillow. When everyone is there: talk and have supper, talk and set up camp in the family room, talk and make popcorn, talk and listen to music, talk and watch the group's favorite movie, and talk and talk until you all fall asleep. In the morning share hot chocolate, juice, doughnuts, and bagels. Then everyone can chip in to pick up the room. Don't forget to thank your friends for coming.

Picnic at the Beach or Park

Invite six friends to join you for a picnic at the beach or park. You'll also need to ask your parents, and one of your friends' parents to help drive and supervise swimming. On the day of the party, pack the picnic lunch and gather towels, beach chairs, sunblock, insect repellent, a battery-operated radio or CD player, and a beach ball. Head out midmorning to pick up your friends. They should bring bathing suits, towels, and any of their favorite CDs. During the day you'll swim, play games, eat, listen to music, talk, and people watch. At the end of the party, the adults drive everyone home.

Miniature Golf Tournament

Invite five people for two teams of three people each. Start with a light lunch at your house—sandwiches and chips—and then head out to the miniature golf course. Play the round and then determine tournament winners (everyone should win something)—lowest score, highest score, weirdest shot, trickiest shot, bull's-eye winner at the end if there is one, best putting form, etc. Give out gag prizes and certificates. Round out the afternoon by stopping for ice cream before you take everyone home.

FOR A LARGE GROUP (EIGHT TO FIFTEEN GUESTS)

Host a Luau

Plan a Hawaiian theme party. Invite ten or eleven friends for dinner from 6:00 or 6:30 to 9:30 P.M. (or a little later, if your parents say okay). Your party invitations can be decorated with palm trees, hula girls, or surfers. Ask all guests to wear Hawaiian-style shirts. You can get tropical decorations from party or department stores. Give your guests a lei as they arrive, set up outside (weather permitting), get a CD of Hawaiian music, and serve Hawaiian food—pineapple, grilled mahi mahi (a kind of fish) or chicken, other fresh fruits, and juices. If you know someone who could teach a few hula dance moves, ask her to join you.

Sports Team Barbecue

If you play on a team, invite everyone over for an end-of-the-season barbecue. Invite the coaches, too. Decorate the party area in the sports theme. Take any articles about your team's season, pictures of team members, and a copy of the season schedule and record, and post them on colored paper. Eat burgers, chicken, or hot dogs cooked on the grill, chips, and fruit salad. For dessert have a big cake, also decorated in the sports theme. If you have videos of the team in action, show them. Plan an informal Wiffle-ball game, or kick some soccer balls around for a little activity. If it rains, break into two teams for a game of Trivial Pursuit—the Sports edition.

Whatever type of party you have, always be sure your parents will be around. While they do not need to participate in the games, they should be present, visible, and available to help out with the cooking, maintaining some order, and dealing with problems if they arise.

> ## MAKE IT A BIRTHDAY PARTY, TOO!
>
> Y*ou can make any of the parties mentioned above into a birthday party. If you do . . .*
> - *Be sure to say so on the invitation.*
> - *Add birthday cake to the menu.*
> - *Remember that your guests will probably be bringing you birthday gifts. You'll probably be opening the presents during the party and thanking each friend for his or her gift right then.*

" *A successful party is one where the guests get along well, the activities are fun, and the food is good.* "

HAVING FRIENDS OVER

PICTURE THIS: Katie and Laura's teacher puts them together as partners for an art project. It is the first year they have been in class together. They discover they like each other, and Katie asks Laura to come over on Saturday. Laura says yes, and they work it out with their parents. What can Katie (host) and Laura (guest) do that will help their new friendship grow?

BEING A GOOD HOST—KATIE

+ **Katie should be ready** when Laura arrives. She should not keep her new friend waiting while she finishes playing a video game with her brother.

+ **Katie should have some activities planned** so they don't sit around saying, "What do you want to do?" "I don't know—what do you want to do?" Instead, Katie should suggest some choices—"I have an album with my art project from last year or some new CDs we can play. What would you like to do?" (This is a new friendship, so any activities that will help them get to know each other better will be good.)

+ **Katie needs to include Laura** in whatever activity is going on. If she is doing a jigsaw puzzle, she needs to ask Laura to join her. "Do you ever do jigsaw puzzles? We do them all the time. Here, you sit here where you can see all the pieces." If Laura says she really doesn't like to do jigsaw puzzles, then Katie should stop and move on to another activity with her guest.

+ **Katie should offer snacks** or a meal depending on the time. Give specific choices. Instead of "Do you want something to eat?" Katie should say, "Dinner's not for a while. Would you like some popcorn or fruit now?"

✦ **Katie should consider Laura's comfort.** For instance, if she notices Laura seems really warm, she should turn down the heat or open a window.

BEING A GOOD GUEST— LAURA

✦ **Laura should arrive on time**—whatever time they agreed to.

✦ **She should be prepared to join in.** If she just says "No, I don't like to do that" to everything Katie suggests, the friendship won't go very far. Laura might even discover a new activity she never knew she would like.

✦ **Laura should be careful** with the things in Katie's house. She should keep her feet off the furniture, ask which glass or plate she can use, and let Katie handle the electronic equipment. If Laura breaks something, she should offer to have it fixed or replace it.

✦ **If Laura needs to use the phone,** she should ask Katie first.

✦ **Laura should offer to help** with clean up: picking up, clearing the table after lunch, or doing the dishes with Katie.

OVERNIGHT VISIT
MULTIPLE CHOICE

WHAT IF . . . *You are spending the night at your friend's house. The whole family is watching a PG-13 movie together. You are not allowed to watch PG-13 movies.*

WOULD YOU . . .

1. Tell your friend you're not allowed to watch PG-13 movies and go read a book while they watch?

2. Call your parents and ask them what you should do?

3. Just watch it and talk to your parents about it the next day, asking them what you should have done?

4. Just watch it and never tell your parents?

CORRECT ANSWER: *1 and 2; 3—maybe; 4—never. The only response that would always be wrong is 4. Only you know which of the others would work for you and your parents. The best bet would be to share this multiple choice with your parents now and decide with them what you should do when you are a guest and your hosts invite you to do something that is not allowed at your home.*

BOTH HOST AND GUEST

Katie and Laura both need to use all the good manners they know. These include the basics of greetings and introductions, mealtime manners, good conversation, sharing, and more. For example, as soon as Laura arrives, Katie must introduce her to her parents and siblings. Laura should ask Katie (and her parents) if she may help with any meals and cleanup. Katie could tell Laura about the family's mealtime routines, and Laura should try to take part in these. When they're talking in Katie's room, they should pay attention to each other (be good listeners!).

OVERNIGHT SPECIALS

If the visit to a friend's is for one or more overnights, there are some other things to know.

Host:

- ✦ Be sure your guest knows your family's routines.
- ✦ Be sure she has a place to put her personal things.
- ✦ Make adjustments for her comfort (if she always sleeps with the light on, provide a night-light).

Guest:

- ✦ There is an old expression: "When in Rome do as the Romans do." It means you should try and do things the way the family you are visiting does.
- ✦ Keep personal things with your overnight bag, not spread out in the bathroom.
- ✦ Let the host know if there are special needs (such as leaving a night-light on).
- ✦ Write a thank-you note after the visit.

WE'VE GOT TICKETS . . .

Going to a concert, recital, or the theater can be an amazing experience. The musicians or actors have spent months, weeks, days, and hours sharpening their talents and putting together a program designed to entertain and excite the audience. The colors, lights, sound, music, costumes, and dance create a performance enjoyed by all. People are there because they want to be—in fact, they have probably paid for the tickets that may have been hard to come by. Just one person can spoil the enjoyment of those sitting nearby—by eating, talking, or fidgeting. When you go to a concert, recital, or the theater, it's important to be considerate of the performers and the other people in the audience.

A QUESTION *for* PEGGY & CINDY

QUESTION: *I went to a concert last week. The kids sitting in front of me talked, giggled, and whispered the whole time. It spoiled a good part of the performance for me. What could I have said to them?*

ANSWER: *You could be in an awkward position if you said something. Those kids already showed they're not concerned with what you or those around you thought of their behavior. It is not likely they would have listened to anything you had to say. Therefore, the best thing you could have done is to ask the manager or an usher to ask the kids to tone it down. Those in charge are the ones who should stop what was spoiling your enjoyment of the event. Other than requesting help with the noise, there's not much else you could have done without possibly causing a big stir.*

SOME BASIC GUIDELINES FOR CONCERTGOERS

✦ **Be on time!** Otherwise, you'll have to climb over people to get to your seat and interrupt others' enjoyment of the concert. (Some theaters won't let you go to your seat until a break or intermission if you arrive after the lights go down.)

✦ **Don't talk to your friends** during the performance. Save it for intermission!

✦ If you need to stand in line for tickets or refreshments, **don't butt in.**

✦ If food and drink are allowed, **eat quietly** and take care not to spill—it is likely to go all over someone else.

✦ **Don't sneak food** or drinks in.

✦ If you have to get up to go to the restroom, wait until it is in between numbers. **Say "Excuse me, please" to the people you have to pass**. Pass facing the stage with your back to the people you are squeezing by.

WHEN YOUR SISTER IS THE STAR

It is especially exciting to watch a performance when you know someone who is in it. It is important, though, to respect her hard work. Catcalls and whistles from you in the audience could be a distraction and may make it more difficult for her to perform. Instead, how about bringing her a bunch of flowers to present to her at the end of the show? She will really love that! And there will always be time to tease her after the performance.

WE NEED REFEREES

PICTURE THIS: *A hockey league in Small Town, USA, was having a terrible time with the referees. All the calls went the wrong way. They missed the fouls, didn't see the goals, missed the offsides, and called penalties that never happened. So the league just did away with the referees. The coaches stopped play when there was a foul. The fans decided if the puck went in the net. And the players called the penalties. How successful do you think it was? Referees are there to make the game proceed smoothly and fairly. The next time you want to yell at the referees, remember Small Town, USA, and show them some respect, instead.*

Concerts, recitals, and the theater can be quite formal. Still, even at less formal events you should use the same manners mentioned here. Whether you're at a ball game, the movies, a circus, or a school play, the people around you deserve your consideration. They will be just as distracted by you climbing over them or whispering and giggling with your friends as your fellow concert-goers. So, whatever the show, be considerate of the others in the audience, and everybody will enjoy the performance that much more.

GOOD SPORTS

What do spelling bees, soccer games, a debate, a tennis match, and an election for class president have in common?

Sportsmanship. Sportsmanship is manners on the field of competition.

Any time participants pit their talents against one another—any time there are winners and losers—how you play the game is as important as winning. Competing is a tricky thing because there are always winners and losers. Players work hard to develop their skills. They want to win. Winning or losing can be emotional. And when things get emotional, manners sometimes get lost.

But manners are what help you get past the emotional moments. Good sportsmanship is simply minding your manners even in the heat of the game. These basic manners will show you how:

✦ **Follow the rules.** Whether you are playing a team game or running for class president, learn the rules and then follow them.

✦ **Don't argue with judges and referees.** They are there to help the game proceed fairly. Sometimes they miss a call. Most times they get it right. But their call has to be the final word and arguing with them will get you nowhere.

✦ **Be considerate of the other players.** Share equipment. Don't get mad and go home with the only ball. Make sure everyone gets a turn. Compliment others on their good plays or work.

✦ **Thank your teammates.** Whether you win or lose the election, make sure you thank everyone who helped with the campaign. If you are playing a sport, thank the coaches, the manager, and the other players on your team.

✦ **Avoid boasting or showing off.** You make others feel bad by trying to make yourself look good. When you do that, *you* don't look good!

WIN OR LOSE WITH GRACE

Nobody likes a poor loser; they don't like poor winners any better. Poor winners and losers alike are usually guilty of putting too much of the emphasis on winning. Enjoy the game; enjoy one another's company; enjoy the satisfaction of using your talents (whether just your own or as a team) to see the activity through to the end. How to be a good winner or loser? It's simple. . . .

Good Winners

- ✦ **Thank the loser** for a good game.
- ✦ **Are happy** about winning but don't gloat.
- ✦ **Avoid overconfidence**—no one bats 1,000.

Good Losers

- ✦ **Thank the winner** for a good game.
- ✦ **Don't pout** and sulk.
- ✦ **Never blame** others for the loss.
- ✦ **Focus on how** they might do better next time.

A QUESTION *for* PEGGY & CINDY

QUESTION: *Sometimes I feel so frustrated when we lose a game because I think the referee only called fouls against our team. Should I say something to the referee at the end of the game?*

ANSWER: *Just play the game the best you can. If the calls really were one-sided, let your coach deal with it. He can talk to the group that manages the referee training and scheduling if it really seems there is some unfairness in the way games are called.*

WHEN YOU ARE A SPECTATOR

Sportsmanship doesn't apply only to the players. When you are in the stands or on the sidelines, you are part of the event. A positive, excited, cheering crowd can help spur their team on to victory. Sportscasters even comment, "That play really got the crowd into the game!"

The important thing is to find the balance between "being in the game" and overdoing it. It's amazing how much one person's behavior can affect how much another person enjoys the event. Manners can help you find that balance, so you can cheer for your team but not ruin the game for those around you.

Good Fans

ALWAYS:

+ Cheer for good plays by their team.
+ Sit down when the crowd around them does.
+ Show support for *any* player who is injured and has to be helped from the field.
+ Use good language when they cheer.

NEVER:

+ Boo when their team doesn't do well.
+ Cheer when an opposing player is hurt.
+ Throw things onto the playing area.
+ Name-call or use foul language when they cheer.

CHAPTER FIVE

OUT AND ABOUT
GOOD MANNERS
MAKE GOOD NEIGHBORS

Consideration is the key to good manners at public fun places. It's thinking about how what you do will affect others.

Robert Frost once wrote a poem saying good fences make good neighbors. Well, that may be true, but good manners also make good neighbors. Whether you live in an apartment, a condo, or a house, manners make life better and easier for everyone. Use of manners should not be limited to family and friends. Neighborhood relationships are important to daily life, so do everything you can to keep them strong.

✦ **Greet your neighbors** when you see them in the morning. Say, "Good morning, Mr. Williams," with a smile.

✦ **Offer to help out.** "You want a hand with those packages, Mrs. Land?"

✦ **Keep the noise down,** especially if it's early, late, or nap time.

✦ **Don't hang out in a big group** blocking your neighbor's walk or the entrance to your apartment building.

GIRL SCOUT COOKIES?

Mrs. Brown lives in your neighborhood. She doesn't have any children but loves to support the neighborhood kids. Her house is full of Girl Scout cookies, candy bars, magazines, and gift wrap. She buys raffle tickets and tickets to shows, gives change to UNICEF, and supports the athletic boosters at the local middle school. And for every time she supports one kid from the neighborhood, five others ring her doorbell.

When you plan your next fundraiser, make a little postcard for Mrs. Brown that says, "I already have my candy bars. Thanks!" If she wants, she can put that on her door so she doesn't have to tell five other kids she already gave. She'll be more likely to continue supporting every project that the neighborhood kids bring to her door if she can do so without being swamped. And, she'll surely appreciate the fact that you all are grateful for her support and are making an effort not to bother her needlessly.

✦ **Ask if you want to do something** that involves going in another person's yard.

✦ **Never go in** the neighbor's house or apartment **without permission.**

RESPECT EACH OTHER'S PROPERTY

WHAT IF . . . *The quickest way to your friend's house is across your neighbor's back lawn. You and your friend go back and forth so often, you notice the beginning of a path.*

YOU COULD . . . Ask before walking on your neighbor's property. Any activity that damages or affects your neighbor's property is inconsiderate. The neighbors may have been making a big effort to develop a beautiful lawn. Talk to them. You'll probably need to change your path. Maybe there's a section of their property they don't care about and you could reroute your path. The few minutes you save by going across their lawn is not worth starting a problem with your neighbor. You have the opportunity here to stop a problem before it starts.

BORROWING AND LENDING

The old proverb says "Neither a borrower nor a lender be." But in communities where neighbors get along, borrowing and lending can be a form of sharing.

"Hello, Jack. Can I please borrow your math book? I left mine at school and I have to study for a quiz tomorrow."

A few basic manners related to borrowing and lending is all it takes to make sure neighbors can thoughtfully take part in this form of sharing.

If You're the Borrower

ALWAYS:

+ Remember that "please" and "thank you" are essential to every transaction.
+ Return the item in the condition you borrow it. If you break it, either fix it or buy a new one. If you lose it, replace it.
+ Return the item as soon as you are finished with it.

NEVER:

+ Assume you can borrow something and take it without asking.
+ Pass the borrowed item on to the next neighbor down the street.
+ Make a habit of borrowing. Once in a while is okay, but your neighbor might begin to resent it if you treat him like a lending library.

DOGS, CATS, AND OTHER PETS

Neighborhood disagreements about pets are often the most difficult to deal with because they involve a furry friend someone—either you or your neighbor—loves a lot. The very best bet is not to let disagreements about pets start or get out of hand. It is hard to believe that not everybody thinks your best friend, Spot, is just about the cutest pet going, but it may be true. Let's consider some of the reasons they may not:

+ Your new puppy keeps racing through their new and fragile flower garden.

◆ Your seven-year-old beloved cat takes up residence under their bird feeder and keeps the birds away.

◆ Your dog barks all day long while you are at school and your parents are at work.

◆ Your two puppies pull their garbage out of the cans and spread it all over their lawn.

◆ Your neighbors are terrified of snakes and live in constant fear your pet boa constrictor will escape even though he never has.

◆ Your exuberant dog jumps up on them every time they walk by. He's not mean, just friendly, but they're a little afraid of dogs.

What should you do? Show consideration for your neighbors. Keep your pets under control. Most towns have leash laws; follow them. Keep your cats in if they disturb the neighbors. (It's a good idea to keep them in anyway. Indoor cats live much longer lives than outdoor cats.) Ask your neighbors if you can show them your system for keeping your snake secure. Consider alternatives to leaving your dog home alone for extended time periods, or find a space in your home where his barking won't be heard next door.

It's not always your pet that causes the problem. What do you do when the neighbor's pet causes problems for you?

A QUESTION *for* PEGGY & CINDY

QUESTION: *The neighbor's dog keeps running over into our yard and pooping. He's a really cute dog, but it makes it hard to play in our yard. What should we do?*

ANSWER: *Ask your parents to help you with the problem. They could talk to your neighbor and ask that he keep his dog out of your yard. Your mom or dad could explain that the dog is leaving a mess in your yard and that people keep stepping in it! Chances are, your neighbor isn't aware of the problem and he'll honor the request to keep his dog home. You all could find out about leash laws where you live, and your mom or dad could also mention the rules to the neighbor. If all else fails, your parent could report the problem to the dog catcher and ask him to find a solution.*

> *Use of manners should not be limited to family and friends. Neighborhood relationships are important to daily life, so do everything you can to keep them strong.*

YOUR EXTENDED HOME

Your neighborhood or apartment building is like an extended family. You practically live with the people next door and down the street for many years. It is important to build strong relationships. Neighborhood cookouts, holiday parties, and support in times of trouble and celebration develop into traditions that enrich community life. Look for ways that you can be kind to your neighbors; you'll be building strong relationships. Remember that good manners make good neighbors.

MALL MANNERS?

Malls must have been created with kids in mind—fast-food courts, music stores, clothing stores, sunglass huts, candy counters, and video-game arcades! The defined boundaries of a mall can help parents feel their older children are safe when they've been left there on their own for a while, and kids get the opportunity to shop independently with their friends.

"Okay, you three can go off on your own. Don't go any farther than the Casual Clothes Store, and let's meet in the food court at noon. That's one hour from now." Or if you're a little older, it might sound like this, *"Okay, you three are on your own. Do NOT leave this mall with anyone besides me. I'll meet you at this entrance in three hours—two o'clock!"*

Just because you've left your mother behind is no excuse to leave your

---

RUDE STORE CLERK

WHAT IF . . . *You have a favorite store at the mall that always has things you really like, but the clerks always either ignore you or follow you around as if they don't trust you.*

WOULD YOU . . .

1. Ask the clerk why he is following you around.

2. Ignore the clerk following you around and just act your best.

3. Stop going to that store. There are plenty of clothing stores you like in the mall.

CORRECT ANSWER.

Don't bother with 1. The confrontation isn't worth the effort. Either 2 or 3 is a good response. Choose the one that suits you.

manners behind. A few good manners will actually make your time in the mall better. When you are polite or friendly to others, they are more likely to help you out or treat you with the respect you are showing them.

FIVE BASIC MALL MANNERS

1. **Make room for the other people who are walking in the mall.** When you walk down the halls, keep it to two or three abreast. A big group of kids walking six across gives the image of a huge snowplow taking out everything in its path.

2. **Watch your words.** Say "Excuse me," "Thank you," and "Please" to clerks, other shoppers, and your friends. When you say "Please" you are asking; when you don't say please, you are demanding. When you say "Thank you" you are showing appreciation; when you don't, you are showing a lack of appreciation.

3. **Volume.** This one is easy: **Keep it down!**

4. **In the food court use only the tables you need.** Avoid spreading all your packages and backpacks over extra chairs and tables. Pick up after yourselves. Clear your trash, put tables and chairs back where you found them, and wipe off the table if you've managed to spill stuff.

5. **Use your basic manners.** Say "Good morning" to store clerks. Smile. Open the door for someone else. Don't bring all your friends in line in front of you. Put things back on shelves and racks as you found them. If you run into a relative or family friend, introduce your friends if they don't already know one another.

FROM YOUR PARENTS' PERSPECTIVE

"Jane and Sally, you're sure you want to go on your own? Okay, you have two hours. Be back here at one o'clock and, please, don't talk to or go anywhere with any strangers and stay in the mall."

No matter how many times you reassure your parents that you can handle this independent time in the mall, they will worry. It's not that they don't trust you—if they didn't, you wouldn't be off on your own. It's just that there are so many things they can imagine happening, they can't possibly ignore them all. If you want to continue with trust between you and your parents, there are several things you can do:

✦ **Be on time to your meeting place!** Every minute you are late seems like an hour to your parents, because they worry about your safety. Be smart, be considerate . . . be on time.

✦ **Stay within the boundaries you agreed to.** If you manage the limits well the first time, your parents will be more apt to expand them the next.

✦ **Share your experience with them.** They'll be so curious as to how it went and what you did. This is a big step for them and they will be eager to hear about it.

✦ **Be aware that your parents have friends who may be at the mall.** Think about how your actions may reflect on your parents if their friends should see you and possibly get back to your parents.

That's it. That's about all it takes to show respect for your parents and yourself. Enjoy your trip to the mall, have fun with your friends, and act in a way that will make sure you can return again.

HAVING FUN IN PUBLIC PLACES

Think about a group of kids going to the beach and deciding to play Frisbee. They notice that there is a family nearby and decide to move down the beach a little. Definitely good manners! And it probably increases their fun, too, since they don't have to worry about kicking sand on people. By being considerate in the first place, the kids increase both their own and the other family's enjoyment of a day at the beach.

There are plenty of places in and around communities designed for physical activities and fun: beaches, parks, skate parks, ski areas, bike paths, ice rinks, bowling alleys, public pools, etc. These areas have several things in common:

✦ People of *all ages* enjoy themselves there.

✦ While there may be some organized team

NIX THE SWEARING

Swear words are said to shock people. The fact is they don't shock. Most adults have heard them a thousand times and are NOT shocked by the words or impressed by the persons saying them. Kids may be shocked the first time they hear them, but it doesn't take long for that impression to change once they have heard them a few times.

activities (bowling leagues or team sports) they have times designated as "public," and people go there just for fun—not competition.

✦ Kids are apt to go there with a group of friends.

✦ There are often snack bars.

Is it possible to have fun and good manners, too? Not only is it possible, the good manners will actually increase the chances for fun for everyone.

CONSIDERATION—THREE QUESTIONS

Consideration is the key to good manners at public fun places. It's thinking about how what you do will affect others. There are many people trying to enjoy the same activities you are enjoying. It's important that you don't create a situation where they aren't able to do so. The best bet is to look around you. Ask yourself three questions:

1. **Is what you are doing going to interfere with someone else's fun?** Have you monopolized the volleyball net so no one else has a chance to have a game with their group?

2. **Could your activity create a problem for someone else?** If you are racing around the rink with your friends, are you risking knocking down a beginner who doesn't have much control yet?

3. **Have you considered your noise level as well as activity?** Is your boom box booming or your voice really loud?

The essence of consideration is to look at the people around you and act in ways that don't hurt others. In the long run, you'll not only make it better for others, you'll improve things for yourself.

A QUESTION *for* PEGGY & CINDY

QUESTION: *We went skiing last winter and there were these two boys who*

PEOPLE WHO CAN HELP

At all public places there are paid staff who will help you out if you're having trouble with someone else at the place. They will also say something to you if you're a little out of line. Be respectful of these folks. Their job is to keep things safe and enjoyable for everyone. The good manners you show them will help them do their job better:

+ **Lifeguards**—They need to focus on the water. Don't talk to them when they are on watch, and if they instruct you to get out of the water, do so without question.
+ **Park rangers**—They are there to keep things safe and to protect the park environment. If you have questions about things you see, ask them. If they ask you to stay out of a certain area, follow their directions as they are probably protecting habitat or have knowledge of an unsafe condition.
+ **Rink attendants**—They keep the ice clean and attend to safety. When they tell everyone to change directions, change directions. And when they ask everyone to leave the ice so they can bring the Zamboni on for cleaning, use the time for a break.
+ **Snack bar attendants**—Especially around lunchtime when everyone is hungry, wait your turn patiently in the line. The snack bar attendants can't make the hot dogs cook any quicker. Grumbling and complaining won't help!

kept crashing the lift line and butting in front of us. What could we have said to them?

ANSWER: *Sometimes all it takes is for you to let them know you're on to their tricks. "Excuse me, but the lift line forms at the end . . . that way!" If something like that doesn't work, don't get into an argument with them. You can tell the lift attendant that the boys are line crashing, and the attendant will watch for them and take care of their behavior.*

FROM THE AMERICAN FOUNDATION FOR THE BLIND
EIGHT TIPS FOR SHOWING SENSITIVITY

When you are with a person who is blind or visually impaired:

1. **Introduce yourself** *so he knows who is in the room or make conversation with him.*

2. **Use a natural tone of voice.** *Don't speak loudly or slowly unless he also has a hearing impairment.*

3. **Speak directly to him**—*not through a companion or guide who may be with him.*

4. **Feel free to use words that refer to vision.** *It's fine to say, "Wait till you see the new school building!" or "Did you watch that special on dogs last night?"*

5. **Feel free to describe things** *referring to color, patterns, designs, and shapes.*

6. *If you see the person about to bump into something, calmly and firmly say, "Wait a minute; there is a chair in the way," and then* **offer to give him a hand**.

7. **Do not pet, feed, or distract his guide dog**, *no matter how cute she is. She is working and it would be rude and unsafe to distract her.*

8. **When you are leaving the conversation or room, make a point of saying, "Good-bye"** *or "I'm out of here—see you later," so he doesn't wind up talking when no one is there.*

DEALING WITH DIFFERENCES

KIDS ARE KIDS

No matter what their abilities or disabilities, kids are kids. They like to laugh, they get tired of homework, they feel angry at their parents, they like to watch television, and, most of all, they like to be with other kids. So when a kid with a disability comes into your class or moves into your neighborhood, the best thing you can do is to ask him to join in. You'll learn the special things you might need to do to make it work. As you get to know him better, you'll soon learn to see beyond his disability and enjoy him for who he is. Before you know it, he'll just be your friend, not the kid with a special need.

Here are some basic courtesies you can show while you learn about the differences your new friend will bring to the classroom or neighborhood:

- **All basic manners apply**—friendly greetings, smiles, please and thank you, and introductions.
- **Don't label people by their disability.** Say, "We have a student who is blind in our class," not "We have a blind student in our class."
- **Offer to help when you can.** Take your cue from the person with special needs or his caregiver. You can hold the door for a person in a wheelchair or who is blind just as you would for anyone. But don't push the chair through the door or grab someone's arm without offering first.
- **Take the time to learn about the condition.** Talk to your parents. Check out the Internet. There are many organizations that provide information for conditions that might require special sensitivity.

IF YOU HAVE A DISABILITY

Many of the kids you meet in school or the neighborhood have no experience with people with special needs. They may not know what they can do to be inclusive even if they want to. They may say or do things without realizing that they are being hurtful or exclusive. That is no excuse, but it may be the reality. You can ease the situation by giving them ideas about how to help. Ask them to hold the door open if you are in a wheelchair. If you are hard of hearing, let them know it's easier for you to understand if they face you when they talk. Explain that you need a few minutes by yourself to take your medication if you have to give yourself insulin. Most of the kids you meet will be glad to help you or to include you in their activities. They simply need to know what you would like them to do.

VISITING IN THE HOSPITAL— QUIET, PLEASE

Visiting people in a hospital or nursing home can sometimes be a little awkward. The setting is filled with strange sights, sounds, and smells. The person you are visiting may not be feeling too well and in need of time for rest and recuperation. Just knowing what to say can be difficult. By doing the following you can make the visit better for both the patient and yourself:

1. **Call ahead and schedule the visit** so you don't arrive just as your friend is going off to be x-rayed.

2. **Keep your visit short.** The person you are visiting is likely to be pretty tired. When she comes home, you'll have lots of time to talk.

3. **If you want to bring your favorite cookies as a treat, check ahead** to be sure cookies are allowed on the diet.

4. **If the medical record is in the room, don't look through it.** Medical records are private and you don't look at them just as you wouldn't read through someone's checkbook if it was on the table.

5. **Quiet, please!** People are in hospitals or nursing homes because they need rest as well as medical care. Many don't feel well. Some older people get confused easily. Keep your voice down; avoid loud, raucous laughter; and don't play a radio or the television at a high volume. If the person you are visiting has a roommate, be especially careful to keep your visit quiet.

A QUESTION *for* PEGGY & CINDY

QUESTION: *I am going to visit my aunt who is in the hospital. Should I bring a gift of some kind?*

ANSWER: *You can always bring a get-well card. Some are pretty; some are humorous. Think about the person you are visiting when you decide which style to bring. Flowers or a small plant can brighten up a drab hospital room. Avoid a huge arrangement. Some hospital rooms are small, and there may be little space for extras. Or your aunt might love a little stuffed animal. The idea is to bring some cheer, not fill up the room, so keep it small and cuddly. If you know that it is okay on her diet, a plate of cookies can be a welcome treat.*

The important thing is that you are visiting. More than anything else you bring, your aunt will enjoy seeing you. So arrive with a smile on your face and some good news to talk about. Your visit will be the best gift you can bring.

KNEEL, STAND, OR SIT?

You're spending the night at a friend's house. The next day you will be attending worship services with your friend and her family. Your own family doesn't attend any worship services, and you are very nervous you might do something wrong.

The more you know what to expect, the better experience you'll have. You also want to feel comfortable with your own actions. Having some idea about what will happen will help you anticipate what to do. There are some things you can do to make it easier:

Ask Your Parents

They may have been to services there or have some friends who attend those worship services. They might know what to expect. Ask them how much you should participate in the service. If you are of a different faith, they might suggest you sit quietly during prayers.

Ask Your Friend

When you are making your plans to stay with your friend, be sure to find out whether you need any special clothes. Does your friend dress up for worship?

Ask your friend what you might expect. Will there be singing? Does she go to any education program? Do kids your age participate in any or all of the service?

Watch Your Friend

Wait to stand, sit, or kneel when she does. If your parents have suggested you sit during prayers, just sit quietly. You don't have to sing, pray, or kneel— especially if any of these makes you feel uncomfortable.

Follow Along in Prayer Books or Hymnals

Most faiths have prayer books or music you can use to follow along. If you understand a little about the service, it will be more interesting for you, and you may learn a little about the religion.

YOU ARE A GUEST

At most religious services there are rituals and orders of worship that are part of the faith. Members of the congregation are at home with the routines. If you attend, you are a guest and should use all the manners associated with being a good guest. The main thing is to act respectfully, even if you don't understand exactly what is going on.

ALWAYS:

+ Talk in quiet, respectful tones when you are in the worship space.

+ Sit quietly during the service of worship.

+ Make sure your clothes are clean, neat, and not torn or full of holes.

NEVER:

+ Wear clothes that are overly revealing. Avoid short shorts or miniskirts, tank tops, or very tight clothes, even when the dress code is informal.

+ Eat candy or snacks or chew gum during the worship service.

+ Run, put your feet up on the furniture, tip back in your chair, or touch items that are special to the faith.

+ Make huge sighs or act bored.

+ Laugh at, make fun of, or complain about any of the rituals and parts of the ceremony, even if your hosts do.

CELL PHONES IN PUBLIC PLACES

CELL PHONE ANARCHY (WHEN THERE ARE NO RULES)

Did you ever wish we could just have no rules, that everybody could do as they pleased? That's what happened when cell phones were invented. No one invented manners to go along with them. People simply use cell phones whenever and wherever they want. Cell phones ring in restaurants, movie theaters, classrooms, and even in church. People have private conversations in public places. Travelers trying to relax at the gate before their flight are treated to all the facts of a broken romance or a pending business deal. It's cell phone anarchy!

Turn It Off!

Cell phones are great! You can let your parents know if you're coming home late and where you are, eliminating needless worry and battles with them. The ability to call someone if you are lost or in trouble is a great safety feature. So it's not a good idea to do away with cell phones, no matter how rude people are with them. The trick is not to be rude.

✦ **Turn it off!** Be the master of your cell phone, not a slave to it. Let your voice mail get messages for you, and then, when you won't disturb others, get your messages and return the calls.

✦ **Give the people around you a break.** If you need to use your phone, move to a corner of the space you're in, to the edge of the hall, or entirely out of the room. Don't come back until you've finished your call and turned off the phone. When you do need to talk on any phone in public, keep your volume down.

✦ **Vibrate.** If you must have your phone on because you are expecting a call, set the ring to vibrate mode. A ringing cell phone is one of the most annoying distractions there is.

✦ **Lower the volume.** When you do need to talk on any phone in public, keep your volume down. There is no need to shout into a cell phone!

CELL PHONES: YES OR NO?

Cell phone anarchy does not work. People become really annoyed with some of the inconsiderate uses of cell phones. Safety concerns have come up. So some places have made their own rules. Below is a list of public places that have rules about cell phones. Be sure to check before you use yours:

AIRPLANES	*MOVIE THEATERS*
SUBWAYS	*CONCERT HALLS*
TRAINS	*THEATERS*
RESTAURANTS	*CHURCHES*

◆ **Avoid treating everyone around you to the details of your personal problems.** "Mom, I'm so mad at Carrie! She told Mary that I didn't . . ." Wait until later when you can talk in the privacy of your own home.

◆ **Don't try to walk and talk at the same time.** If you need to make or take a call, stop your activity, complete your call, and then go back to what you were doing. When you talk on the phone, it takes concentration and you could easily walk right into other people on the sidewalk. Even though a walking accident might not be as bad as a car accident, you could hurt yourself or someone else because you were concentrating on a phone call. And forget about cell phone talking while crossing the street.

Remember, all the manners associated with telephones apply to cell phone use (see pages 53–54). These additional guidelines just extend the consideration you should apply to regular phone use to your use of a cell phone.

IN A LOUD VOICE

When you have a conversation, you have many clues to help you understand what the other person is saying: shaking or nodding heads, facial expressions, moving lips, eye rolls, and hand gestures. On the phone, any phone, those added clues are missing. Add the fact that cell phone users often are sure that the person on the other end of the call can't hear them well. So what happens? People talk louder. And it's noise galore!

Another volume phenomenon is when the listener can't understand what the other person is saying, he tends to talk louder:

> *"I couldn't hear what you said."*
> *"Xccsxxchh ccchsxxx."*
> *"WHat???"*
> *"Xccsxxchh ccchsxxx."*
> *"I COULDN'T HEAR WHAT YOU SAID!"*
> *"HOW'S YOUR BROTHER?"*

And you are both shouting when the real problem was a bad cell-phone connection. If you are in a public place, everyone around you is treated to your frustration and probably to the details on how your brother is. That's because you are not likely to lower your voice again, even though you understand what the caller is asking.

CHAPTER SIX

ON THE GO— AWAY FROM HOME

PLANES, TRAINS, AND AUTOMOBILES

"Whether you're in a car, plane, or train, the trip will be as good or as bad as you make it."

You're headed off on a summer vacation trip of a lifetime. The only thing is, the first twenty-four hours will be spent either in a *car* with your parents, your sister, the dog, and all your bags and camping gear (your only break—eight hours in a motel sleeping in a double with your sister), or on an *airplane* packed in with 230 other people (you'll spend three hours in an airport in the middle of the night), or in a *train* car with 35 other people all trying to sleep sitting up. Close quarters for an extended time can be stressful. What can you do to make it easier?

PLAN AHEAD

Pack a backpack with things you can do in a small space:

+ **Books,** comic books, and magazines that you will enjoy. Nothing passes the time more quickly than getting lost in a great story.

+ **Games**—travel bingo, your Game Boy, travel Battleship, a magnetic chess or checkers set, a deck of cards.

+ **A writing kit**—stationery that you've personalized with stickers or printed out on your computer, fun postcards, extra stickers, several different colored markers and pens, envelopes, stamps, and an address book.

+ **Drawing or crafts kit**—paper, markers, colored pencils, and drawing pens.

+ **Discman,** headphones, and your favorite tapes or CDs.

Help your parents put together a bag of food and beverages.

+ **Any snacks** that you all like: pretzels, potato or tortilla chips, crackers, and nuts.

+ **Fresh fruits**

+ **Avoid foods with strong smells**—Limburger cheese, for instance.

+ **Juice,** sodas, and water

Ask your parents to make a copy of the travel itinerary for each person, so everyone can keep track of the trip without having to ask when the next stop is fifty times.

During the trip, think about the other sardines traveling with you.

TAKE A BREAK

During the trip you may have a chance to stretch your legs—at an airplane terminal, a railroad station, or a rest area. The following four tips are things to consider during these welcome breaks:

1. **Restrooms**—If there is a line, wait patiently. Pick up after yourself by wiping the sink and making sure paper towels wind up in the bin.

2. **Make room for others**—At the gate or terminal, don't put your bags up on chairs. Other travelers would like a place to sit also.

3. **Walk, don't run**—you're not on a ball field. While it feels good to stretch your legs, keep the pace at a walk.

4. **Escalators**—It is definitely a challenge to try to go up the down escalator or walk against the direction of the moving sidewalks, but an airport is no place to play. If someone gets hurt, your travel plans could be delayed.

PICTURE THIS: You're trying to get a little rest. You know sleeping will help the time pass quickly. The trouble is the person behind you is swinging his legs out of boredom and kicking the back of your seat. Then he stands up to go to the restroom (plane or train) and he pulls himself up on the back of your seat. It's difficult enough to sleep, and a fellow traveler is just making things worse.

Don't do the same to another traveler. Avoid kicking, pulling, and pushing other travelers' seats.

PICTURE THIS: There is an empty seat between you and the next person. The next thing you know her books, papers, lunch, and Discman are all over the seat crowding you just as if someone were sitting there.

Keep your mess from spilling over into other travelers' already limited space. If there is an empty space, share it with the other person, don't hog it for yourself.

PICTURE THIS: You and your brother are having a nice time playing magnetic chess. It takes some concentration. A group of kids on the other side of the aisle are playing music, talking loudly to one another up and down the aisle, and laughing really loud. How irritating!

Talk quietly with your family and travel friends. You don't want to treat everyone else around you to your conversation.

PICTURE THIS: You've been in the car for eight hours; your little sister starts whining, "When are we going to get there? I'm hungry! I'm bored! Why didn't we fly?"

Whining can really add to everyone's stress. Try to keep that in mind the next time you are feeling bored, hungry, and ready to be at your destination.

A SMILE AND A PLEASANT VOICE

Whether you're in a car, plane, or train, the trip will be as good or as bad as you make it. There can be a ton of inconveniences when you travel, including delays, changes in schedule, crowds, weather problems, and other things you might not even imagine. Your parents, the customer service people, and the other travelers are all in it with you. *A smile and a pleasant voice can make all the difference.* You may not be able to change the weather, but you can make the unexpected stay in the motel an adventure rather than a disaster. Although some things may be out of your control, you can choose your reactions. And to a certain extent, you can choose what the experience will be like for everyone with you. Which will it be?

YOU'RE THERE!

Room 524 overlooking the pool! It's taken twenty-four hours of grueling travel to get here, but this is it! A whole week stretches out before you. Maybe it's Cabin 32 on the E deck or Rustlers Cottage at the dude ranch. But this is vacation. You're here with your parents and two sisters, and the deal is to relax and have fun.

BOREDOM IS NO EXCUSE

One morning a guest was in the shower in her hotel room. Through the noise of her shower, she could hear the game of hockey going on in the hall. It was a continuation of the game started the night before. It's hard to play hockey quietly. Those kids decided to relieve their boredom by playing a game, but they spoiled the other guests' quiet time. That was not okay. Boredom is no excuse to be inconsiderate of others.

SHARED SPACES

PICTURE THIS: You and your sister are walking back to your room. Suddenly, she says, "Race you!" and heads down the hall at a dead run. Just as she turns to see how close you are, another guest steps out into the hall. Oh no!

It's not just the danger of an accident. There is also the noise factor. The other guests in the rooms along that hallway probably were treated to the sounds of the race. In a hotel there are shared spaces: the restaurant, the gift shop, the lobby, the elevators and/or escalators, and the hallways. Tempting as they are, they are not designed to be play areas for kids. Be considerate of other guests and play in the places designed for it—such as the pool area, fitness room, game rooms, or outdoor play areas.

HIDDEN PLEASURES

You already know about the activities that you can do that will make this a great week. Swimming, riding, snorkeling, hiking, fishing—the list goes on. Maybe there are some other benefits you haven't thought of. Check out the following three ideas of things to add to your list of vacation activities:

*1. **Talk to your family.** Traveling is a great opportunity to reconnect with your family. At home your lives are filled with friends, school, work, and activities. Use this time to get to know one another better. Enjoy one another's company. Maybe you didn't know your dad was a champion diver in college. You might discover something you have in common with your older brother that you never realized.*

*2. **Include time to read** during your vacation. With no phone calls from your friends to interrupt, you might have some time to discover a new author or maybe an old one. One kid we know "discovered" mystery writer Agatha Christie. She wrote sixty-six books and once he discovered her, he knew he could keep right on reading her books for a very long time.*

*3. **Take the opportunity to try different foods.** Whether you are in a different country or a different part of this country, there will be local treats to try. Don't pass them up for the familiar hot dog. You might even want to try cooking this new treat when you get home.*

A HAPPY STAFF MEANS A HAPPY GUEST

Whether you are at a hotel for one night, or a resort, cruise ship, or ranch for a week, there are many people working to make sure your stay is a good one. Some you see; some you don't. There are some things you can do that will help make their jobs more enjoyable. If you make their jobs more enjoyable, it is highly likely they will make your stay more enjoyable. Think about it. A happy staff is likely to mean a happy guest.

✦ **Observe those basic courtesies:** smiles, greetings, please, and thank you.

✦ **Neaten up after yourself.** It isn't fair to ask the maid who makes up your room to have to work around your dirty clothes, all your stuff, and half-eaten snacks.

✦ **Follow posted rules** and instructions. If you miss one and a member of the staff points it out to you, follow the instructions from then on. Don't get mad at the staff person. It's his job to let you know.

✦ **Let someone know when you really like something**—such as it's the best hamburger you ever had. Ask the waitress to tell the cook.

EATING OUT—FROM FAST FOOD TO FINE DINING

What does eating out mean to you? Maybe you picture sitting in your car, ordering at the drive through, and picking up your food at a drive-in window. Or, perhaps you envision standing in line at one of five registers trying to keep track of how fast your line is moving in comparison to the others. Other kids might see a family style restaurant where the menu includes word puzzles, jokes, or other table activities. Maybe your vision is of an elegant restaurant with candles, white tablecloths, and linen napkins.

Eating out is all these things and more. It may be a special treat that just happens once in a while or part of a trip where every meal is "out." The point is the meal is not cooked in your kitchen, someone else serves it up to you (this can be at a window or at your table), you don't wash the dishes, and you pay for it.

A QUESTION *for* PEGGY & CINDY

QUESTION: *You have to use your manners at a fast-food restaurant? You've got to be kidding!*

ANSWER: *Think about it. There are lots of manners in fast food. For the most part, they are the common courtesies you use in lots of other settings.*

✦ **Waiting in lines requires patience.** Don't jump from line to line. If you're stuck behind someone who is ordering for ten people, you can move over to the end of the next line, but don't keep switching, and don't invite your friends to cut in front of you.

✦ **Choose one line.** Some people think it's really clever to stand in one line and have a friend stand in the other. Then whoever gets there first orders for both. This can be really annoying to the others standing in line. Don't do it!

✦ **Use the line time to decide** what you want so when you get to the front of the line you can order quickly.

✦ **If you are ordering for several people, make sure some of them are there** to help carry your order to the table.

✦ **Pick up after yourself**—both at the counter where you get ketchup and mustard and at your table. At a fast-food place, the deal is you clear your own table.

✦ **If you spill something, let the staff know** so they can mop it up.

✦ As always, **use common courtesies!**

> *Sometimes people forget and leave their table manners at home when they go out. But table manners are universal.*

SIT-DOWN RESTAURANTS

Whether it's a fancy five-star or a family style restaurant, courtesies are the same. Once you're seated, you'll have a chance to look over a menu, order what you want, have some time for table conversation, and enjoy a meal prepared, served, and cleaned up by someone else. There are some "always" and "nevers" based on consideration and respect that will make your meal more special than ever:

ALWAYS:

✦ Make an effort to join in and be social. Even if the restaurant was not your first choice, make up your mind to enjoy it. Eating out is special and your attitude will affect everyone's experience. Make it a good one.

✦ Use the glass(es) on the right-hand side of your setting and the bread plate on the left.

✦ Put your napkin in your lap as soon as you sit down.

✦ Be respectful to the waitstaff whether you're placing an order, requesting something special, or pointing out a problem.

◆ Ask to be excused if you need to go to the restroom.

◆ Push your chair in when you leave the table to keep the spaces between tables clear for other customers and waitstaff.

NEVER:

◆ Order more food than you're hungry for. (If you're served more than you can eat that's one thing, but don't order many courses if you can only eat one.)

◆ Play with your food or beverages.

◆ Leave the table without being excused.

◆ Act in a way that will disturb other diners—loud, raucous behavior, cell phones on, hyperactivity.

Whether it's a fancy five-star or a family-style restaurant, courtesies are the same.

A QUESTION *for* PEGGY & CINDY

QUESTIONS: *What if your food's cold when it's supposed to be hot? What if you get the wrong food? What if there's a fly in your soup? What if it's way too spicy? What if . . . ?*

ANSWER: *If there is any problem with your food, let your parents (or the host if you're there with friends) know about the problem. They can call the waiter over and either describe the problem or ask you to describe it. Most restaurant staff will do what they can to make it right. They want your experience to be a good one so you'll come back. If it's just that you don't like what comes, but it is what you ordered, then the problem is yours and you should just leave what you don't like on your plate without further comment.*

TABLE MANNERS

Sometimes people forget and leave their table manners at home when they go out. But table manners are universal. (You can review the table manners section in the At Home chapter before going out to a restaurant.) Dining out is the classic social experience. On one hand, rude behavior can spoil it quicker than anything else. On the other hand, courteous behavior will enhance the experience and make it the best! Once again, you have some control here. What will your experience be the next time you go out?

CAMP HAVAGREATIME

Camp Havagreatime has been around for eighty-five years, but this is your first summer going there. It's actually your first time going to camp anywhere. While many camps have their own special traditions, there are some that fit at any camp. Here's a "manners journal" that will help you out with your camp experience wherever that may be.

GETTING READY

During the few weeks before camp, check the lists they send you and make sure you have the things you need. If Camp Havagreatime asks you to limit your gear to one duffel, a backpack, a sleeping bag, and a pillow, don't decide to make it two duffels because you can't live for two weeks with the stuff that fits in just one. The limits were probably set because the cabins there are small and that's all the space you'll have. Make sure you do bring all the things they suggest. The staff design the list to make sure everyone has everything that he or she'll need.

CREATE A CAMP CORRESPONDENCE KIT

Here's a pre-camp activity to fill your time while you're waiting to head out.

1. **Find a box or Baggie** *that is big enough to hold paper, note cards, envelopes, pens, an address book, and stamps but small enough to tuck into a duffel or on a shelf. Decorate it. Include your name so counselors know whose it is in case you lose it.*

2. **Make a list of all the people you'll write to**, *with your parents at the top. Grandparents, aunts, and uncles all love to hear from their young relatives at camp. Add three or four of your good friends to the list. And your brothers and sisters would be both surprised and pleased to be included in the mail call. Gather addresses for everyone.*

3. **Collect all necessary supplies.** *Design your own stationery or postcards by creating borders and adding you name. Make sure you have plenty of envelopes. Different colored pens and pencils make writing more fun.*

4. **Go to the post office and buy stamps** *from among the great variety now offered. Stamps should go in the kit the minute you get home.*

5. **Address some envelopes or postcards before going off to camp** *so you'll have everything ready to write on.*

Now when you're at camp, it will be easy to send a quick note home. And writing to people is the best way to get mail in return!

ARRIVAL DAY

When you get to Camp Havagreatime, the first thing you'll do is check in. You'll be assigned to your cabin, you'll meet your counselor, and before you know it, you'll be saying good-bye to your parents. For some kids this is the hard part. Just look around you. You'll probably see some kids who look as if they don't want to say good-bye to their parents at all. The camp will have lots of activities planned to help you through this time, and before you know it, you and the others will be experienced campers.

Choosing Bunks

At most camps, it's first come, first served. If you arrive late and the only bunk left is the bottom one behind the door, it's yours. You want to start off on the right foot. Smiling, going with the flow, and making an effort to see the bright side of things will establish a good impression, one that people will have for the next two weeks. It is your choice. Make it a good one.

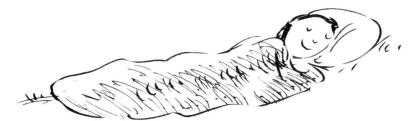

MAKING FRIENDS

One of the really special things at Camp Havagreatime is the opportunity to make new friends. The camp will help you out by putting you with a group that is your same age. The fact that you're all at the same camp means you're interested in some of the same things. Keep in mind all the things you already know about making and keeping friends and you'll do well at camp. A short review might help:

+ **Smile, greet everyone** cheerfully, and use those "magic words" such as please, thank you, you're welcome, and excuse me.
+ **Respect other campers' property**—don't borrow without asking or go into other campers' duffels without their knowledge.
+ **Be honest.**
+ **Be ready to take part in activities** whether they're new to you or you've done them for years at home.
+ **Show what a great time** you are having by smiling and participating.

A QUESTION *for* PEGGY & CINDY

QUESTION: *I was at camp last summer and one of the other campers was really homesick. I heard her crying in her bunk the first night. What could I have done?*

ANSWER: *Loneliness, being in a strange place, being emotionally or physically tired, and being separated from people you love sometimes add up to homesickness. You could have talked to the camper and offered support. "Is there anything I can do?" Then, the next morning asked her if she felt better. If not and you continued to hear her cry, you could have talked to the counselor. She is trained to help kids who are homesick and would appreciate hearing from you if she was not aware one of the campers was experiencing this difficult reaction to camp.*

DAYS TWO TO THIRTEEN

Activities are scheduled from wake up to lights out. Participate! Counselors are there to help you have a good time, but they can only provide the opportunities. You will decide how you will take advantage of them. Get to know different campers in the different activities. Try out new things. The way to find out if you like archery is to try it. This is your chance.

Sometimes things don't go just perfectly. A week of rain can dampen any camper's enthusiasm. The "bug juice" (canned fruit juices served at every meal and snack) may really be bland. But tough circumstances sometimes make great experiences. You'll all laugh on the final night when you recall the water pouring through your cabin door after three days of rain. Or you'll all groan together when you get served that last glass of juice. So grin and bear it. The grinning together part is what you'll remember.

LAST DAY

It's hard to believe two weeks went by so fast. Now it's time to say good-bye. There are all kinds of manners associated with this last day.

- ✦ **Thank your counselors** and other camp staff.
- ✦ **Get addresses** of all your new friends.
- ✦ **Introduce your new friends** to your parents—and meet their parents.
- ✦ **Pack up your stuff**—leave nothing behind so your bunk area is ready for the next camper.
- ✦ **Final hugs**, tears, and good-byes!

Your first year at Camp Havagreatime is over. Maybe you'll return, maybe not. But if you gave it your best effort, participated with enthusiasm, and treated everyone else with courtesy and consideration, you'll have an experience you will always treasure.

FIVE COMMON CAB COURTESIES

Because they are expensive, you may not ride in cabs regularly, but here are five tips for the times you do:

1. **Always get in and out on the sidewalk side** of the cab.

2. **Slide all the way over** to make room for the people you are riding with.

3. **If you are giving the directions to the driver, speak clearly** and loud enough so he can hear.

4. **If others are giving the directions, stop talking** so the driver can hear.

5. **Remember your common courtesies**—especially "please," "thank you," and voice volume.

Getting a cab can be quite an experience and people have many tales about rude, pushy people they have encountered while trying to get a cab. The important thing is not to be guilty of such rude behavior yourself. If someone is already on the corner hailing a cab, move down away from the approaching traffic a few feet, so it is clear the other person was there first. Once he gets his cab, move closer to the corner where he was standing.

SUBWAYS, BUSES, TAXIS

SUBWAY CIVILITY

Oh no! You are in the back of the subway car. It is rush hour and the car is PACKED. At each stop you've been pushed farther and farther from the door. How will you ever get to the door and out when you reach the next stop? You could shove everyone and shout, "Move out of my way!" It might work, but you will have added to everyone's stress by about one hundred degrees. Instead, you can just say, "Excuse me. This is my stop." And gently push your way through the crowd. Everyone will understand. They need to get on and off also and face the exact same dilemma.

And that's not all. Whether it's rush hour or a quiet time of day, riding on the subway or metro or underground or whatever you might call it can be challenging. It's rather impersonal the way people have to push, rush, and pack in together. Sometimes you even have to spend one or two hours every day in close quarters with complete strangers. These dos and don'ts have come about as the ways we can make this activity just a little more civil.

✦ **Stay to the right;** on the stairs or moving through the passageways to different trains, keep to the right.

✦ **Have your tokens or pass ready** when you get to the turnstile.

✦ **Wait for people to exit** before you get on.

✦ **Offer your seat** to anyone who might have a difficult time standing—such as someone with a lot of packages, an elderly person, a person carrying a small child, or a pregnant woman.

✦ **Be careful with your backpack.** It's easy to knock into someone behind you and never even know.

✦ **Don't horse around** on the subway platforms.

✦ **Don't lean up against the pole** as if it were the wall. That makes it difficult for anyone else to hold on.

✦ **Don't put your packages on the seat next to you** unless there are many empty seats in the car.

BUS BEHAVIOR

Many school districts in the country do not offer transportation services and kids ride public transportation to school. City bus services provide an efficient, inexpensive way to get about town, whether you're going to school, work, or play. The dos and don'ts for using public bus services are similar to those for subways. But if you picture a crowded bus—that's when manners are the most important—some specifics for bus riding come to mind.

PICTURE THIS: It is 8:00 A.M. and you are at the bus stop for your morning ride to school. People in line include some other students, four people on their way to work, a lady with two preschool-age children, and a man with a cane. What are the manners riders can use to make this morning ritual work smoothly?

Although there are similarities, the list of dos and don'ts for bus behavior is a little different from the ones for subways.

SIMILARITIES:

✦ **Have your bus pass or exact change ready** for the driver when you get on.

✦ **Wait for people to step off** before trying to get on the bus.

✦ **Don't use seats for your backpack** or packages if the bus is crowded. Keep them on your lap.

✦ **Offer your seat** to someone who might have more difficulty standing than you.

✦ **Take care that your backpack doesn't swing** around hitting people behind you.

✦ **Don't horse around** at the bus stop. Wait quietly.

DIFFERENCES:

✦ **People waiting for a bus tend to queue up.** That means they form a line. If there's a line, get in it, and wait your turn to get on.

✦ **If all the seats are taken, move to the back of the bus** to stand. This will make room for others.

CHAPTER SEVEN

OTHER SPECIAL OCCASIONS
WEDDINGS

Speak with your parents or another adult you're comfortable with, and they will tell you a bit about what to expect.

There's a wedding invitation in the mail! And your name is on it, too. Just ask friends, and they'll probably tell you about the fun they had while attending a wedding. Weddings have so much tradition and ceremony, there are books filled with guidelines for the bride and groom and their guests.

YOU'RE A GUEST

Look to your parents or other adults to help you with "wedding-guest manners." And use these tips for being a good wedding guest:

♦ **Respond to the invitation,** letting the bride and groom know whether or not you will attend. There may be a response card with the invitation that your parents will fill out for all of you and return. That's one of the "rules" of weddings because the bride and groom need to know just how many people will be attending. They need to plan for the ceremony and reception (party) afterward.

R S V P		
	FRENCH	**ENGLISH**
R	*Répondez*	Respond
S	*s'il*	if it
V	*vous*	you
P	*plaît*	pleases
Répondez s'il vous plaît = **Please respond**		

✦ **Send a gift to the bride and groom.** Your invitation will probably be included with your parents. They'll know about the custom of wedding gifts, but since the gift will be from all of you, maybe you can help pick out the present.

✦ **Be on your very best behavior**. The bride and groom should be the center of attention, not a young guest like you. During the marriage ceremony and when toasts are given at the reception are special times for quiet behavior.

✦ **Congratulate the bride and groom**. If there's a receiving line, go through it, watching what the adults do. Be sure to shake hands with all the people in line. Look them in the eye and smile as you say "Hi" or "Hello."

✦ **Thank the hosts of the celebration for having you.** That's usually the bride's parents, but check with your parents to be sure exactly who you should thank.

YOU'RE IN THE WEDDING!

Sometimes a bride asks her younger sister or cousin—or maybe her fiancé's younger sister—to be a junior bridesmaid. That is quite an honor!

Boys also might be asked to help out in an important way, such as handing out wedding ceremony programs or guiding people to the guest book for signing. For that special time when you're a junior wedding attendant:

◆ **Your main duty** as a junior bridesmaid is to walk down the aisle (in what's called the processional) before the bride's entrance at the wedding ceremony. You'll wear a dress and shoes like the bridesmaids and carry a bouquet of flowers. You may or may not stand with the couple and other bridesmaids during the exchange of vows. If not, you'll sit with your family or with someone else you know. During the rehearsal, you'll be told exactly where to sit. If you do stand with the others during the wedding, you'll walk out with them in what is called the recessional.

◆ **The "special helper" boy**, who's older than most ring bearers (who are traditionally three to seven), is to stand at the main entrance and hand out programs to the guests as they arrive. Or, he might show people to the guest book after the wedding takes place.

◆ **Junior attendants** are expected to attend the rehearsal, and possibly the rehearsal dinner (usually these occur the evening before the wedding). During the rehearsal, you'll run through the whole ceremony so you'll know just what to do on the day of the wedding.

◆ **The parents of a junior attendant** are expected to pay for their child's special outfit, whether it's a junior bridesmaid dress and shoes or a suit that is similar to what the ushers wear.

A QUESTION *for* PEGGY & CINDY

QUESTION: *I am so excited! I'm going to be a junior bridesmaid in my cousin's wedding. I've been invited to a shower. What is a "shower"?*

ANSWER: *Needless to say, it's not a gentle rain. The idea is to have a party for the bride where the guests "shower" her with gifts to help her set up her new home. Sometimes it's a kitchen shower—then the gifts are all things that would go in her kitchen. If the invitation doesn't say anything specific about a theme, the gift you bring can be anything that will go in the bride's new home.*

WHEN SOMEONE DIES

One morning you get to school and your teacher tells you that your friend's father died during the night and she won't be in school for a few days. You all knew that her father was ill, but you are still surprised and not sure what you should do. You know your friend must be very sad right now. Your teacher helps you all write a sympathy note to your friend. Your parents may suggest you go to the funeral.

It is very likely that sometime before you're an adult, you'll be attending one or more funerals or memorial services. You might feel a bit nervous— especially if you've never been to one—but try not to be. A funeral or memorial service is a special occasion to honor someone's life, and it is a time to comfort the people who are sad about the death of the person they loved. Speak with your parents or another adult you're comfortable with, and they will tell you a bit about what to expect.

A funeral takes place in a house of worship or a funeral home. The service can be a way of helping the family and friends of the person who died. People spend time remembering special things about the person who died. Sometimes family members actually say a few words about the person, helping everyone recall happy times. Gathering together to remember the person's life also gives those who are left behind a chance to think about their own lives and spiritual beliefs. During the service, it's expected that you'll be quiet—sitting still and not talking. Watch the adults you're with. They'll help you follow their lead.

Wherever the service is held, some people may be crying. You, too, might feel like crying. Go right ahead. It's a sad time. Don't worry about your or others' tears. Crying is a natural way for people to grieve, and it can make them feel better.

You'll also notice that people will be greeting one another with quiet kind words and hugs. After the service, there may be a receiving line or a reception. If you find that you are greeted by some of the deceased's family members, don't worry. Sometimes it does feel a little awkward, but your friend will be thankful that you came "to pay your respects" and will probably tell you so. You don't need to say much. In fact, a simple "I'm sorry about your father" is plenty. If you feel comfortable, you could add something kind about him. ("I always loved it when he drove us to our soccer games.")

If it is one of your own family members, and you are in the receiving line, all you need to do when someone says she was sorry to hear about your relative is say, "Thank you." You can add something like, "We're all going to miss her."

The thing to remember about funerals is that they are really part of our lives. For many, many years funerals have given people a way to say good-bye to someone who has meant much to them. And those left behind after someone has died find it's very helpful to be joined by people who offer sympathy, hugs, and kind remembrances.

COMING-OF-AGE CELEBRATIONS

A RELIGIOUS CEREMONY AND A PARTY

Coming-of-age ceremonies have been celebrated in cultures around the world for hundreds of years. They mark the move from childhood to adulthood, at least in a religious tradition. If you're invited to a friend's coming-of-age ceremony and party and you're not a member of that religion, you might feel a little anxious. The more you know what to expect, the less anxious you'll be and the more you'll enjoy the party.

No matter what the religion is, think about these guidelines as you get ready to go to your friend's coming-of-age event:

✦ **Follow the customs of the religion when deciding what to wear.** Ask someone familiar with the religion about head wear. In a Jewish synagogue boys are expect to wear a yarmulke. Usually there are some available for guests at the entrance to the worship space.

✦ **Leave religious jewelry or symbols of a different faith at home.**

✦ **During the service you can follow along** in the Bible or prayer books provided or simply sit quietly.

✦ **Congratulate your friend** at the reception after the service.

Confirmation

In the Christian faith, once children have reached a certain age they usually attend a series of religious classes with other kids their age. When they have completed their studies, members of the group are then welcomed into the church by their minister or priest in a confirmation ceremony. Families and close friends attend both the ceremony in the church and the party. Whether you're one of the "confirmands" (a boy or girl who is being confirmed) or you're attending someone else's confirmation, there are two things to keep in mind:

1. **Confirmation is a religious occasion**, not a big party. While it is a joyous time, it is celebrated quietly in the church, so put on your best "church" behavior.

2. **Churches usually have a simple reception afterward**, serving punch and cake. This reception is sometimes followed by a small gathering of the confirmand's family and close friends for a meal. Those there might give the newly confirmed girl or boy a small gift.

Bar Mitzvah and Bat Mitzvah

MR. AND MRS. GERALD COHEN

JOYFULLY INVITE YOU

TO WORSHIP WITH THEM AT THE BAR MITZVAH OF THEIR SON

MARTIN SETH

SATURDAY, THE FIFTEENTH OF MAY

TWO THOUSAND AND FOUR

AT TEN O'CLOCK IN THE MORNING

THE SCARSDALE SYNAGOGUE

2324 EAST POST ROAD

SCARSDALE, NEW YORK

AND TO CELEBRATE WITH THEM

AT THE RECEPTION IMMEDIATELY FOLLOWING

WILLOW RIDGE COUNTRY CLUB

EASTCHESTER, NEW YORK

RSVP

53 HARRISON AVENUE

SCARSDALE, NEW YORK 10583

For thirteen-year-olds of the Jewish faith, the religious celebrations of the bar mitzvah (for boys) and the bat mitzvah (for girls) are among the most important events in their lives. The student works very hard during the year learning required Hebrew text and preparing to lead parts of the religious service. It is quite an accomplishment, and the celebration following the service is truly a joyous event.

The bar mitzvah or bat mitzvah takes place on the first Saturday (Sabbath) after the boy's or girl's thirteenth birthday. The purpose is to welcome the young person as an adult member of his or her congregation. The ceremony is usually followed by a reception right afterward at the synagogue.

Later in the day of the bar mitzvah or the bat mitzvah, there is often a big party hosted by the teen's parents. Relatives, friends, and classmates of the family and boy or girl are invited by way of a printed invitation. These parties are often big and fancy, with dancing and either dinner or lunch. Everyone invited to a bar mitzvah or bat mitzvah is expected to take or send a gift to the teen, who in turn sends a thank-you note to each person.

Bar mitzvahs and bat mitzvahs are special events. When you attend one, you will soon realize that the religious ceremony calls for respectful quiet. The big celebration later in the day is a time to use good party manners while having lots of fun.

Quinceañera

A quinceañera is the celebration of a Latino girl's fifteenth birthday. You might be invited to attend the celebration of an older sister's or friend's *quince* (short for *quinceañera*). Sometimes there is a Catholic ceremony in her family's church, but there's always a party to honor the girl's passage into womanhood. The party is usually a formal one, with dancing—including the birthday girl's special dance with her father. She also receives gifts from the guests, which she opens and thanks them for later. This is a time for celebration and enjoying a special event together with family and friends.

Emily with her great-grandson Billy, 1946

INDEX